"Brad Moore possesses something  rare as time goes on: courage. Th like he has, looking to God for str has inspired me to remember that but instead life is set up to draw me to the Lord where i do ..... happiness."

Ron Brown
Running Back Coach for the University of Nebraska

"Brad is a survivor and his cancer victory brings courage and inspiration to us all. I'm glad he decided to write his story because it is a clear example of how a "never give up attitude" can make a real difference in whatever a person might face. It is also appropriate that Brad is giving recognition to those who supported him throughout his decade long battle. I remember the incredible support base that held him up during all those treatments, trips and struggles and how that base proved to be larger and stronger than anyone could have ever imagined. Make no mistake however, in many ways; this story is about Brad's mother Diane as much as it is about Brad. For years, we watched in awe how Diane willed her son back to health. I have never seen a mother so committed, selfless and determined to beat this awful disease. How incredible it is that only recently, Diane herself discovered that she too must battle this same awful disease. With Brad, Lee and Kristin's help, we all have confidence that she too will beat cancer as well. The Moore family is a close, loving family who know firsthand the weight of life's biggest battles and have come out on top. The Moore's have been and continue to be an inspiration to us all."

Harlen Wheeler, former Pastor, Church of God

"Brad Moore inspires me to enjoy every moment in life. If most people in life had his faith and attitude, our world would be a much better place."

Charlie Granade, Pastor of Ridgeview Bible Church

"Like many cancer victims, Brad's story shows what a life changing event it is in a person's life. This book captures how he relates sports stories and games with all the turmoil of his cancer. Through his association with my son Josh, he has become part of the McLain family and frequently travels with us to ball games. We appreciate the perspective he has given to us."

Jerry McLain, MD

Brad has always been an amazing young man and nephew. I've had the privilege of seeing him grow up and watched as his interests and talents have developed. I was at the hospital the day he received his first cancer diagnosis. I saw how he stepped up and supported his mother as she tried to absorb the news. I admire his attitude and perseverance as he conquers each hurdle before him. He is a courageous young man, who is an inspiration to not only the family, but all who get to know him.

Sharon Eberly
(Aunt Sharon)

I am so proud of Brad for following his heart and completing this book. What an incredible accomplishment! There are times, no matter how we toil, when words can not express the depth of one's heart, strengthen another's resolve or lighten their heavy burden. But a prayer . . . can rally brave souls, uplift courageous sprits and recharge our faith to battle the insidious enemies . . . like cancer. The 'Healing Prayer' is my offering to Brad when in need of healing and hope.

'Healing Prayer'
The Power of prayer surrounds you and is never ending . . .
Its light blazes bright and never dims . . .
May its strength and warmth sustain and heal you.

Tricia Moon-Beem
(Aunt Trish)

There Is "Moore" to This Story

Senior Class Picture 2001

One young man's true-life account of the struggles
he had with **CANCER**

BRAD MOORE

WESTBOW
PRESS
A DIVISION OF THOMAS NELSON

WestBow Press books may be ordered through booksellers or by contacting:

WestBow Press
A Division of Thomas Nelson
1663 Liberty Drive
Bloomington, IN 47403
www.westbowpress.com
1-(866) 928-1240

Because of the dynamic nature of the Internet, any web addresses or links
contained in this book may have changed since publication and may no
longer be valid. The views expressed in this work are solely those of the
author and do not necessarily reflect the views of the publisher, and the
publisher hereby disclaims any responsibility for them.

Any people depicted in stock imagery provided by Thinkstock are models,
and such images are being used for illustrative purposes only.

Certain stock imagery © Thinkstock.

ISBN: 978-1-4497-3381-0 (sc)
ISBN: 978-1-4497-3380-3 (e)

Library of Congress Control Number: 2011962119

Printed in the United States of America

WestBow Press rev. date: 12/15/2011

Dedication Page

This book is dedicated to the entire Rushville High School
Class of 2001, a great group of friends whose kindness and
thoughtfulness I will never forget.

and

To my mom,
who was, and still is, a committed mother and my best nurse
through all the tough times I had. But most of all,
she is my best friend.

Brad Moore

Foreword

This is not a smooth, easy story with romantic twists and heroic locations. It is a ragged, raw and unembellished story of a young man and his fight with cancer-not just one cancer, nor even two; but rather three different malignancies over a three year period. His story is related in near-diary form which chronicles not only the fears and pitfalls that accompany cancer, but also the everyday events and passages which helped him maintain his balance and equilibrium in this vertiginous and dangerous world. From his numerous and nauseating bouts with chemotherapy to his multiple aggressive surgical interventions, One follows Brad Moore on a journey that few of us can imagine, let alone tolerate.

Having a malignancy in a 17 year old boy is uncommon enough, but not rare. To have a second and different cancer simultaneously is almost unheard of. But to experience a third malignancy within a three year period is impossible to comprehend. Three different cancers in three years time—how could this happen? One can only theorize a complete and catastrophic collapse of Brad's immune system. With the loss of immune competence, new cancer cells could arise in any organ system and grow unrecognized and unchecked—in Brad's case, non-Hodgkins Lymphoma, testicular cancer and thyroid cancer. In truth, with the diagnosis of Brad's last malignancy, we all felt that it was simply a matter of time before a cancer arose which we could not control.

But if such were the case, why then, following his last cancer, did no other malignancy appear? He has now survived 7 years without recurrence or the onset of a new malignancy. Perhaps even more mysterious than his history of three cancers is the fact that no more have appeared and his immune competence is again intact. The physicians and nurses who cared for Brad and loved him treated him with the most modern and up to date methods and drugs; perhaps we did beat the cancers. But we did not, nor could we ever, make his immune system reawaken and flourish. That is the province of God.

In a quiet, ordinary way, this portrait of Brad and his battle with cancer is full of amazing strength and resilience, remarkable perseverance and incredible courage. There is no doubt that the love and devotion of his family and friends helped Brad survive this period in his life. All those around him contributed to his recovery from his bubble gum blowing aunt to Ron Brown the running back coach of the Nebraska football team. It was all the small, ordinary everyday things that helped Brad along and buffered the horribleness of his cancer and its treatment. That is what life is about. That is what love is about.

W. M. Packard M.D.
(Brad's oncologist)

In January 2000, Jerene's sister called. She had received a somewhat frantic phone call from Brad's Grandmother. Brad's grandmother asked if we could help her daughter Diane, to come along side them when they are in Denver. She explained that her grandson Brad needed treatment for cancer. Jerene knew Diane as they both attended the same church in Nebraska as children. Well God gave us both a desire and a peace about helping this wonderful family. God's hand was in this, as we bonded and became extended family during our many trips to the hospital with them. It doesn't seem to us that we did very much, but we enjoyed doing what we did. We were always impressed at the way Brad endured his treatments. He very rarely complained and he always seemed positive about the outcome. He projected to us, "It will be OK." We remember Diane's extreme devotion to her son through it all. She wouldn't leave his side, she didn't even go to the cafeteria to eat, and she never left him! Brad's sister, Kristin, never complained about her brother getting extra attention, and she always gave us her sweet smile. Brad's dad, Lee, came along whenever he could, he was there with strong support. We had fun times too! We were able to attend a Denver Nuggets basketball game, and at least one Colorado Rockies baseball game. We all enjoyed eating out together after the treatments, and even though Brad didn't feel very well, he was always able to help us pick a restaurant. We always remember how God helped them afford a replacement van when they really needed it. God put us together, God made the time with them special, and we are thankful to God for memories we will always cherish.

Joe and Jerene Langfield

I remember December 31, 1999, being pretty much the last of what I call a "normal day." The next day was New Year's Day, 2000. A lot of people were concerned with what the new year of 2000 was going to be like and were talking about all the changes. But I had other things I was dealing with.

This was just the beginning of what would be the biggest change of my life. Here I was, just seventeen, when most kids are living up their youth in high school. I, however, was faced with the life-changing news that I had cancer—yes, cancer. I don't even remember being sick for more than three days in a row in my lifetime. Now I was looking cancer straight in the eye. But I never believed that cancer would win!

The following is the story of my struggles, what I was facing, how I dealt with cancer, and how I want to be an inspiration to others faced with a cancer diagnosis. If I can be of encouragement and support to any one person, then that alone would be my wish.

> One day this disease will be cured for all
> then I can stand proud and tall.
> My courage and strength will endure
> until the times comes for a miraculous cure.
> Until then, I keep a positive attitude
> and fill each day with a lot of gratitude.
> When I cannot dance, then I will sing a song,
> for happy things will makes me strong.
> So I will keep the faith, hope and love,
> and I look for the blessings from above.
> This, my friends will be my answer,
> on how to deal with this thing called cancer.

Chapter 1

A Little about Me

My life began on Tuesday, January 4, 1983, at 6:04 p.m., just moments after an episode of *Wheel of Fortune* had started. I weighed in at nine pounds five ounces and measured twenty-one inches long. My parents, Lee and Diane Moore, named me Bradley Ray. I was the New Year's baby at the Gordon Memorial Hospital, Gordon, Nebraska. I was born just three days after Nebraska beat Louisiana State University, 21-20, in the 1982 Orange Bowl. That is what started me out on the path to becoming a true full-blown Husker fan! My parents received many gifts and baby things for having the first baby of the year. My mom always told me I was special. I was their first child. Three years later, on April 29, 1986, my sister, Kristin LeAnn Moore, was born. My family would then be complete.

When I was born, my parents lived on a dairy farm, south of Hay Springs. While I was just a year old, they moved to Rushville, which is where I grew up. I started kindergarten in 1989. That year, I was selected to be a ring-bearer at the high school's homecoming. It was the highlight of my first year in school. My classes throughout grade school and high school were always pretty small. Five of us started kindergarten and graduated from high school at the same time.

I was just your average student. At first, I had trouble with school, but it got easier as I got older. My memories of grade school were good. Throughout my younger years, things were easy and fun. During the summer, I rode my bike to the swimming pool and went swimming every afternoon. The town of Rushville, where I grew up, was a fairly small town. You could ride your bike everywhere and get from one end of the town to the other end in less than a half hour. I always rode my bike everywhere I went, until I was old enough to drive.

During my younger years, I was also active in Boy Scouts. My parents were the leaders of Boy Scouts the years I was in the troop. In the summer of 1996, our Boy Scout troop, including scouts from Gordon, went to Laramie Peak, Wyoming, for a camping trip. As some of the boys in our troop were sitting around the campfire, we started roasting marshmallows. Well, some of them must have been bored with marshmallows, because they started roasting Tootsie Rolls. I happened to be sitting by Jared Roffers, who was one of the scouts roasting the Tootsie Rolls. As he leaned over to show me this red-hot Tootsie Roll, some of it dripped on my arm. "Ouch!" That was some excruciating pain! It gave me quite a burn! I was jumping around and screaming. I ended up with a permanent scar from that experience. And to think that I was on a Boy Scout camping trip. They were supposed to practice safety and always "be prepared." The Boy Scout leader said it looked really bad. I was nearly sent home because of it. It's a good thing they never contacted my parents or else my mom would have driven straight to Laramie Peak to get me! My painful little episode ended up earning me a lot of badges while I was there. Overall, it was a good experience for me, with the exception of being burned, and I have good memories of my trip and something about a "Tootsie Roll," that I will never forget.

The next few summers, I was active in 4-H. My friends and my cousins, Connie, Jodi, Jamie, Julie, Jesse, Ona, and I, all had 4-H projects. I did everything from showing a pig to cake decorating. I even baked some biscuits that made it to the state fair in Lincoln. My Grandma and Grandpa Cerny let us keep the pigs at their house.For my family, 4-H was a big event, including the fair and rodeo. So there would be rodeos, concerts, and carnivals all happening the same week. It was right before school started in the fall, so it was everyone's last mini-vacation. My family and I usually took part in the whole week and had a lot of fun.

Later that fall, I started junior high school as a seventh grader. I tried out for football and made the team, but I wasn't very good at it. I remember wanting to play defensive back and the coach telling me that the only place for me was the offensive line. I did not want to play offensive line, but I did, even though the plays were hard for me to understand. Our team won just a few games each year. When I was an eighth grader, I was more experienced at football but still didn't get much playing time. My best memory of junior high football was a game in Gordon my seventh grade year, when I finally got some playing time. During my eighth grade year, the hardest game of the season was the game against Chadron. We tried to keep up with a very fast team.

Entering my freshman year of high school, I went out for football again. I played on the junior varsity team. One key memory I have was a game against Hemingford. I still did not completely understand the offense and blocking assignments. I missed my block, the quarterback was sacked, and the coaches yelled at me because of it. I started to realize that not everyone was cut out to play sports when I was sidelined after that play. I finished out the season, but I knew that some people are meant to be fans, and I was definitely one of them.

Rushville is very well-known across Nebraska for its wrestling team. Over the years, Rushville has won seven state championships and was runner-up several times too. Some of the Rushville wrestlers still hold individual and team records in Nebraska's state high school record books. So I tried out for wrestling my freshman year. I weighed in at 145 and never had to diet to keep my weight. Since Rushville was so good, I never was considered for the varsity team. I wrestled junior varsity instead. In practice, I was matched up with Mike Johnson, the lightweight wrestler, with a weight of 103. He was also a freshman and my classmate. We were always matched up together. I really did not know what I was doing as far as wrestling was concerned. He knew all of the fundamentals and was pretty good. But since he did not even weigh 103, he was not strong enough to really do anything with me. He still was able to beat me pretty easily. When it came time for the wrestling meets, I would get beat all of the time. Even in three overtimes, I seemed not to be able to come out on top. My record ended up being 0-21. At the end of the wrestling season, at the Actives Banquet, I was awarded with Perfect Attendance for practice and got the Effort Award for the year. Again, I realized that I was just a fan of wrestling too.

Since playing sports seemed to not be my thing, I answered an ad in the local paper to be a carrier for the *Omaha World-Herald*. I had not been sixteen very long and had just received my driver's license. My first car was a brown, four-door 1979 Chevy Nova. It was not pretty to look at, but I bought it with my 4-H money that I had saved up. I started delivering the *Omaha World-Herald* in the mornings before school. The paper route took about forty-five minutes. I soon had the route memorized, and it was a piece of cake to do. My mom would help sometimes, as would the rest of my family, so they would be familiar with the paper route too.

In the summer of 1998, a brand-new grocery store opened up. It was called Ryan's Market. I got a job there right away as a carry-out boy, working after school. I was doing a paper route in the morning, going to school during the day, and then finishing the day working at the grocery store after school. I would get home around 7:00 p.m. It seemed like a lot to handle, but it really wasn't too bad, and I liked that I was earning my own money.

My sophomore year came and it soon was time for football season. I went to all of the pre-season practices, but when the season started, I told the coaches that I would not be participating. The same was true with wrestling. I became a big-time sports fan more than ever. I would even travel to the away games and support the team. The football coach loved my interest in football and was shocked at the depth of my sports knowledge. The head coach at the time was Kelly Stouffer, an ex-NFL quarterback and a Rushville native. He would quiz me about football trivia and I would often be able to tell him the correct answers.

During my junior year, while on the 1999 Christmas break, the new millennium was soon coming, and the Church of God youth group was putting on a lock-in for kids at the church to go to and have a safe, fun-filled New Year's party. This was held at the Clinton High School. A while before I went to the New Year's party, I had an unusually stiff neck. I did not think anything of it at first. I remember telling my mom that it was stiff and that I felt some pain, but we did not do anything about it at that time. I went to the lock-in and met up with some friends and played basketball most of the night. My sister and I stayed until the clock struck midnight and the New Year began. We then went home, and I went to bed, with my neck still hurting.

Chapter 2

The Year 2000

On New Year's Day, I woke up still having a sore neck, but my family and I went to watch college football games at Marvin and Janet Coat's house in Gordon. Later in the evening, when it was time to go home, my neck was not any better, so since we were already in Gordon, my mom insisted I go to the hospital and have it looked at.

Well, this is where my story starts to get ugly. We arrived at the hospital emergency room and told the doctor on call that my neck was sore. She started pushing on my neck really hard and asked me where the pain was. She thought I had swollen thyroid glands and said it was not my lymph nodes. I passed out shortly after she started pressing on my neck because of how hard she was pushing. I guess I was doing some pretty weird things because she overreacted and thought I was having a seizure. She admitted me to the hospital, and I was put in the Intensive Care Unit with a heart monitor for the first night. The doctor also ordered me to take anti-seizure medicine that first night. Then, she also performed a spinal tap on me. She did not do it right the first two times, and after the third attempt, it was finally done. When I woke up, I had a very bad headache and backache because of the incorrectly performed spinal tap. She did not even allow my parents to be in the room when this procedure was being done.

I was pretty much messed up at this point. I spent the night in the ICU and tossed and turned all night long because I was in so much pain. That night, there was a lady who died, a man came in having a heart attack, and the New Year's baby was born, so there was a lot happening at the Gordon hospital. My mom stayed with me during the night. The next day, I was still in the hospital for more tests. Later in the day, they put me in a hospital room, and I remember watching Nebraska playing Tennessee in the Fiesta Bowl on January 2. That night, Darrell Johnson, who was my church youth leader, came in, visited me, and stayed for the game. He came to be my support and encouragement. Nebraska ended up winning the game 31-21. The game was very important for me to watch, but because I was in so much pain, I really did not have a chance to watch it closely, so it was taped for me. On January 3, I was still in the Gordon Hospital and was feeling somewhat better, but they wanted to do more tests. Mom stayed with me the whole time, except for that Monday morning, when she went home really early to do the paper route for me. The nurses came to my room and took me down the hall to the X-ray department where Kim Roffers worked. She did an ultrasound and had Dr. Hutchins come into the X-ray room to overlook the procedure. That is when they found abnormal lymph nodes.

The doctor who had first seen me in the emergency room said she thought I had a thyroid problem, then a seizure, then performed an awful job of a spinal tap, and put me on anti-seizure pills, and put me in the ICU that first night with a heart monitor. She obviously did not know what she was doing. Later we found out she no longer works there. I will always give credit to Kim Roffers and Dr. Hutchins for checking into things further. Since this ultrasound showed abnormal lymph nodes, my parents wanted our family doctor, Dr. Hutchins, to take over my treatment, and he did. He said

I needed a CAT scan. After the CAT scan, Dr. Hutchins said I could go home but I needed to be back later that day for surgery. He said they would need to do a biopsy on one of the abnormal lymph nodes in my neck. After the surgery, I was really happy that the hospital staff was letting me go home. I was really looking forward to being home for my seventeen birthday, which was the next day.

I only got as far as the front door of the hospital and then I got really sick. My mom went and told the nurses what happened, and I was then readmitted to the hospital. At first, they thought I got sick just because I had not eaten in a while. So, the nurses brought me some soup and I was able to eat some. I did feel better after I ate. Then the nurses got orders from the doctor that they could let my parents take me home for my birthday. It was not much fun because I was in a lot of pain. If I laid down, my back would kill me, and if I sat up, it felt like hammers hitting my head. I was in so much pain; I could only stand it by being doped up on pain pills. On the day of my seventeen birthday, Pastor Wheeler came to see me, along with Grandma and Grandpa Cerny, Aunt Sharon and Uncle Leon, and some family friends. Then somehow, people heard what happened to me and just came over to show their support toward me and my family. Even a lot of people from the Church of God came to visit. It was really cool. I was told there had to be close to a hundred people that visited that day and night. Our house was full and overflowing. I really never had any idea of how many people were actually there because I was still in such horrible pain from the spinal tap. (I was really too sick to even sit up in bed.) Later, my family told me the whole driveway was full and the highway was full on both sides. It was lined with cars for a whole block. I was later told that I also had a birthday cake made for me with my picture on it, but I was way too sick to care.

The College Football National Championship Game was also the night of my birthday. But since Nebraska had already played the night before, this would not have been a "must see" game for the normal person. But I am not the normal person. I am a football freak. I still could not sit still long enough to enjoy that game either. But thanks to VHS technology, it was also taped for me. I told my mom that I wanted to spend the whole night at home. Around 11:00 p.m. that night, I could not take the pain any longer. It hurt to sit up. It hurt to lie down. I was in terrible pain. My mom and dad made arrangements for someone to take care of Kristin and then took me to the emergency room in Gordon. We were all glad that Dr. Hutchins was on call. After arriving at the ER, Dr. Hutchins gave me a blood patch. He took blood from my arm, put it in a syringe, and put it in my spinal column to "seal the leak." He said I was suffering from a spinal leakage. I immediately felt relief from my severe headache, but my back still hurt quite a lot.

I had a biopsy taken from my neck on January 5, 2000, and then was released from the hospital soon after that. The doctor said it would be a few days before we could find out the results. Later that same day, Dr. Hutchins called my mom and asked us to meet him at the Rushville Clinic. That is when he told us that the test showed large-cell lymphoma, and told me I had *cancer*. He told my parents and I to go home and get some things and head to Scottsbluff right away. He had already called ahead and told Dr. Packard we would be on our way there. So, after my mom totally fell apart and cried with my dad, along with friends and family who came to support us, we left for the trip to Scottsbluff, a two-and-a-half-hour drive. On the way there, I was in so much pain. I could not lie down or sit up without feeling really uncomfortable. I had to have my dad stop the van several times to readjust. At first

I was trying to lie in the back of the van but couldn't stand the pain; then I tried the front seat, even facing the rear, with my knees on the floor board, trying to make my back pain go away. It was awful It was the longest two-hour drive I ever went through.

As soon as we got to Scottsbluff, Dr. Packard met us at the emergency entrance. He looked at me and said I was a mess. He gave me something to take away the pain in my head and back. Then he put me in an office chair with rollers, pushed me to the MRI room, and gave me a tour of the hospital. That night I felt I was in much better hands with him as my doctor. He truly cared about me. I had the MRI done the next day. The surgeon, Dr. Forney in Scottsbluff, told me that because of my cancer, it would benefit me if I had a port inserted in my chest so they could give me chemotherapy drugs that way. It was so that they did not have to poke me in the arms all the time. This was called a groshong. The doctor inserting the groshong into my chest really helped me. This was my second of many surgeries that I would have to have.

On January 7, I was feeling a lot better. The MRI test results came back and confirmed what Dr. Hutchins had told us: it was cancer. I finally got to eat a good meal that day. I was very hungry. I remember I had fried chicken from the hospital and a delicious whopper from Burger King. Food never tasted so good!

I was first told I had Burkitt's lymphoma. Dr. Packard thought I had a kind of cancer that was very rare and thought it would be best to send me to Presbyterian St. Luke's Hospital in Denver, Colorado, where they specialize in pediatric cancer patients. Neither my parents nor I had ever even been to Denver before. So my dad asked Uncle Martin and Aunt Louise Atkinson, who lived near Scottsbluff, if they would help us drive to Denver for the first time. They drove since my parents were not in any shape to drive. They were pretty shook up with all of this news of me having cancer. My mom especially was taking it very hard.

Dr. Packard & I in Scottsbluff

The following is a copy of what was printed in the *Omaha World Herald* daily newspaper:

"Students Help Ill Classmate"

"When Brad Moore found out he had cancer, his friends from Rushville High School banded together to help out with his paper route. When I heard that, I thought wow, what a good bunch of friends. Then I realized, this was a morning paper route. These teen-agers were getting out of bed around 4:00 A.M. to make sure Brad's customers received their papers on time. What a great bunch of friends. Brad first noticing pains in his neck at the end of December. By New Year's Day, the pain was so severe that his parents took him to the hospital in nearby Gordon, Nebraska. For six days, Brad's doctors couldn't tell the

Moore family what was wrong. Brad was worried about his World—Herald route in Rushville. He had just started the job in October, and he didn't want to lose it-especially after all the nice notes and tips and gifts his customers had given him for Christmas. "We had a friend," said his mother, Diane, "a good friend", offer to handle it for a few days. "We didn't anticipate any of this."

"Friend In Need"

On January 6, doctors removed a lymph node on Brad's neck and told his family that Brad had lymphoma. His family was shocked. "It's just not something a mother thinks will happen to her kids," Diane said. "It's a mother's worst nightmare." Brad was sent to a hospital in Scottsbluff and then to Denver. His family went with him. And his paper route was up in the air. The friend who was doing it ran into one of Brad's classmate's parents at the grocery store. "The junior class wants to do something for Brad," the mother said. "What can we do?" That's how the juniors landed the paper route. "In our world history class," said junior Jared Roffers, "we just all volunteered to take a different day. It took just a few seconds, and all three weeks filled up." Most people were glad to help Brad. "He's the nicest guy you could ever meet," Jared said. Besides Jared, these Rushville students lent a hand; Mike Johnson, Zack Kearns, Ryan Hunter, Tonya Heath, Scott Hunter, Troy Reeves, Jed Taff, Shae Higgins, Court Feddersen, John Abold, Carlos Ferreira, Jackie Thies, Matt Jansen, Jerry Bagola, Bill Lattin, Mike Bourne, and Jon Henry. That's most of the junior class and a foreign exchange student from Brazil. "The first day, it took me an hour and a half to do it," Jared said. "I think it usually took Brad 40 minutes." The job went faster when they went in pairs to share the work. To get the papers out on time, someone had to be at Brad's house every morning at 5:15. "Some kids live 40 minutes from town," Jared said. "and had to get up at 4 in the morning to do it."

"Friends, needed"

Brad and his parents, Diane and Lee, finally came home on Jan. 20. Brad has started chemotherapy. He still goes to Denver once a week for treatment. His doctors are optimistic, Diane said, and so far, Brad hasn't had any major side effects from the chemotherapy. He's nauseous sometimes and really tired. He kind of missed his 17th birthday on Jan. 4, so he had a makeup party on Super Bowl Sunday. "I was feeling pretty good," he said, "so I got to have some friends over." Brad goes to school when he feels up to it. He already has enough credit to pass his junior year, and his teachers are being understanding. "They just said 'Get well and worry about it later.'" The Moores resumed the paper route Monday. Brad really wants to keep the route. He'll deliver papers when he can, and his family will help out on bad days. They can't thank the juniors enough. It was such a relief, Diane said, when they volunteered to help out. But it wasn't really a surprise . . . that's just the kind of kids they are. They're a close class, Brad agreed, and they help each other out. "I've known most of them since kindergarten."

. . . .

On January 8, I arrived in Denver for the first time. First, we met with three doctors who were specialists. Next, we talked with a Dr. Mattous, and he said this type of cancer was very treatable. But just to make sure, he wanted another CAT scan. The scan showed the cancer was growing very fast. It had changed from 8 cm to 9 cm since I had left Gordon. He was not even sure I had Burkitt's or large-cell lymphoma. Burkitt's was more common in African Americans. So the doctors were beginning to think I had a different type. They said I could just have a free day, so they could work on the treatment plan and decide exactly what type of cancer I had, and they would start chemotherapy the next day. January 9, we were still waiting on the doctor to determine how to treat my cancer. It was a very long day! All I could think was, *Why is this happening to me?* I was so healthy my whole life. Having cancer really shocked me, and I just wondered how I was going to respond to the chemotherapy.

On January 10, the doctors performed a bone marrow biopsy. The procedure was like taking a cork screw and driving it into my hip bone. They said they got a good sample. Later that day the doctor thought I should be moved into the B part of the hospital, as they still were not sure what type of cancer I had. So I moved out of my room and into another. This room was for more serious patients. Anyone who came into this room had to wash their hands, wear a mask, and be careful what they brought into the room. It was a very big room and was very nice for Mom because she had a couch that turned in to a bed. We also had a bigger TV than the other rooms. It was great for my sports watching, and I liked that room because of the larger TV.

Dr. Cullen came to see me and discuss my treatment plan. By the time Dr. Cullen got there, the stitches from the biopsy that was done in Gordon were almost bursting from swelling and the cancer. All the doctors gathered in my room trying to decide what type of cancer it was. This took almost five days.

Finally, later that day, Dr. Cullen came to me and told me that it was Lymphoblastic lymphoma, T-type, but they would know more by morning. I was really glad the doctors took all this time to really do research to discover what type of cancer it was. Otherwise it would have been harder to know what form of chemotherapy to give me.

My mom looks back on this time and just wonders how we made it through it. There was so much going on and so much to absorb. Just the news of me having cancer was such a shock in its-self. Then on top of that, being faced with all the news that I would be getting chemo treatments was overwhelming and so hard to comprehend, especially to Mom. She was by my side twenty-four hours a day and seven days a week. It was so hard for her to understand why this was all happening to me. This affected not only me but my whole family. They all suffered along with me.

By January 11, Dr. Mattous came to visit and said that he would be turning my case over to Dr. Cullen. Then we met with Dr. Cullen and he said he was 100 percent sure it was lymphoblastic lymphoma and that they needed to get started right away with chemotherapy treatments. So they gave me some drugs to get me ready for the next day. That day, I took a walk to the children's cancer center. It was called the CHOA clinic which stood for Childhood Hematology Oncology Associates. It was really sad to see all the kids there who had cancer. There were little kids carrying around IV poles, and their hair was completely gone. It was very scary and sad because I was just starting with my treatments. Those kids had already been through so much. My mom got very emotional and it was hard for her to see all the cancer patients there and know that I would soon be facing the same thing. It was hard for all of us. I had just turned seventeen at the time and the doctors called that age a gray area because eighteen is considered an adult but sixteen was a child still, so I got lucky. I was treated as a pediatric. I probably got better care because of that. I felt like I was treated pretty special by all the nurses there, as they were used to taking care of much younger patients than me.

I had my first dose of chemotherapy on January 12. My youth pastor came to visit me in Denver and then later took Kristin back home with him so she could go back to school. Some other friends of the family came to visit too. One of my classmate's parents, Tom and Kim Marcy, even brought my PlayStation to me. As a teenager who was going to be stuck the hospital for a while, that was very important to me. My friend and former classmate, Kent Janicke, lived in Denver and came to see me that day too. I was given permission to leave my hospital bed for a while, so we took a walk around the hospital building. It was hard to believe I was in Denver and even harder to believe that I was sick. We talked about why this was happening to me. No one could come up with any reason.

The doctor came to visit and had some tests results from the Gallion test. It showed some spots in the stomach and liver area but he did not seem too concerned and said, "We are going to beat this, Brad." He was also pleased with the bone marrow results too. The doctor said I could be discharged to outpatient care. So, we made our fourth move within the Presbyterian St. Luke's hospital in Denver. We moved into Park Manor, which was an outpatient hotel attached to the hospital. This was where Dad and Kristin had been staying. Joe and Jerene Langfield came to visit us and brought me a TV with a VCR. I was able to hook up my Play Station. They also brought a fridge too. We got a few groceries after that. Joe and Jerene are very special people who helped me and my family all the time when we had to be in Denver. Jerene is a longtime friend and former neighbor of my mom's family, and a sister to Jerry Scott. Jerry and Sue Scott are some special family friends also. Joe and Jerene ended up helping us so much. My mom says they are truly angels from heaven, and I think so too! They would come to see me in the hospital every day and keep my mom company during my long surgeries. They would also take us places in Denver, like really nice restaurants and the ESPN Zone too. It was not that my mom did not want to take me places; it was just that she was scared of getting lost in a big city like Denver. She would never drive anywhere but straight to the hospital and straight home!

School had already started in the second half of my junior year of high school. I was not there that much at all. My sister Kristin tried to go to school, but she missed a lot of days too because of wanting to be with the family. It was really hard on my mom to be away from home for such a long time. Kristin really tried to live a normal life, go to school, and do the day-to-day things, but it was extremely hard on her as well.

January 14, I was able to sleep in a bed that was not a hospital bed for the first time in a while. Later that day I got to have my stitches out from the surgery done back in Gordon. Joe and Jerene came to visit the next day, and they took us sightseeing. They took us to Red Rocks Amphitheater. That is where some big-name concerts are held. More important, I was out of the hospital! Some other friends, John and Ila Bishop, from Cheyenne, Wyoming, came to visit, and they took us out to eat. (We went to Hooters. I got my picture taken with all the pretty girls there.)

January 17, I got dismissed from the hospital, and we stayed in a hotel room near there. I was treated as an outpatient for the rest of my chemo treatments. It was like a Ronald McDonald House, where families of sick children were able to stay. I had eight days of chemo, and then on January 20, the doctors said I was going to go home to Rushville very soon. We just had to get an X-ray first. The doctor looked at it and said it was really good, because the cancer cells were reduced drastically. The nurses all stood around the X-ray chart on the wall and were clapping and cheering because it showed signs of improvement! All my mom could do was stand there and cry. I'm sure she was happy about my cancer shrinking, but it was all so much to handle. I was told that the cancer in my neck and chest was the size of a basketball when I first got to Denver.

I was given chemotherapy that day before I left for Nebraska. This certain chemotherapy was called Vinchristine. It was bright red going through my IVs and so the doctors at Denver called it my Husker Power chemotherapy. All of the doctors and nurses knew that I was a big-time Husker football fan. Being in Colorado, I got razzed a lot from the nursing staff about Husker football. They were always teasing me about Colorado and Nebraska being such big rivals. Friends and family back home had gotten me great big Nebraska helium balloons that stayed with me even when I transferred to different hospital rooms. It was my dad's job whether he liked it or not, to carry those giant balloons from room to room. Being in Colorado, I got noticed for having Nebraska Husker stuff, like my ball cap and coat and most all of my clothes, so the nurses all had fun giving me a bad time about being a "Husker Fan." After I got my Husker Power chemo, my mom and I packed to go to Scottsbluff, Nebraska, for the night. I was to meet with Dr. Packard for my treatment plan there too. Dr. Packard was happy to see me. He even met us outside to help make sure I got in okay. He was very caring and he was the best doctor ever!

It was January 21 when my mom and I made it home for the first time since January 8. There were "Welcome Home" signs on the house that some friends put up. It definitely was a nice gift. It felt really good to be home in Rushville!

My 1st day back from Denver "Welcome Home Party"

Soon after that, everyone in town heard that I was home. I began to have several visitors at my house, asking a lot of questions. When the doctors sent me home, there was actually a lot that I still had to do. The Denver nurses brought my mom into a room and told her that she would have to turn into a nurse because she had to take care of my Groshong every day, to keep it clean. Also I was to take several chemotherapy pills every day, and my mom did her best to try to deal with and learn what the Denver nurses were telling her. She was completely overwhelmed and very nervous about dealing with all the daily routine care of my Groshong. It was a lot for her to learn and understand!

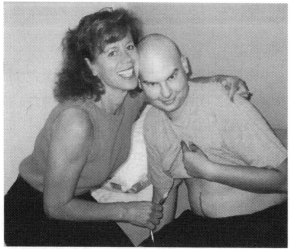
My favorite Nurse Vicki giving me Chemo

I remember one of the nurse's names was Vicki. She brought in a large box of medical supplies, including packages of syringes, bottles of heparin, gauze pads, alcohol swipes, tape, etc. She put the box down in front of my mom and started telling her what she needed to do and proceeded to do a demonstration on me of what my daily routine would be. My mom just stood there and started crying. She said, "I can't do that!" Then Vicki was very stern with her and told her she would *have* to learn how to do this. This was just the beginning of the lessons my mom learned on how to deal with my cancer and the treatments I would be getting. She later had to learn a whole routine of what medications I would take on a daily basis as well, and how to give me shots, which was especially hard for her to do.

I still did not go to school very much at all. I was only home for a few days at a time; the rest of the days, my mom and I were on the road going to doctor's appointments, either in Denver or Scottsbluff. At the beginning of my treatments, I was going to Denver twice a week and Scottsbluff three times a week. So my mom and I were only home on weekends. Then we did it all over again, week after week! This continued for five weeks. We continued making trips to my doctor's appointments. The months went by. My mom and I made most of those trips all by ourselves. During this busy time, my mom would try to go to work whenever she could.

My mom was the one who I depended on during those tough times. She and I became very close. I really can't say enough about the wonderful mom that I have. I am truly lucky to have such a caring mom who would drop anything to take care of me. I love her so much.

The chemo treatments would often include a spinal tap. Since I had such a bad experience with a spinal tap before in Gordon and had those terrible headaches and back pains, I had to trust that this nurse would know what she was doing! I dreaded that so bad! She happened to be my doctor's wife, so I was hoping she knew how to do them well. She never messed up on a single spinal tap, and I had plenty! The spinal taps were important because the doctors wanted to keep the cancer from reaching my spine.

One of the drugs that I had to take was a steroid called Prednisone. They actually put me on this drug to boost my immune system in order for me to be able to tolerate all the chemo they were giving me to fight off my cancer. It was this drug that eventually caused all the damage to my hips and knees. The doctor assured us that if I had not had the Prednisone, I would not have been able to tolerate the doses of chemo they were giving me—I would not be here today, writing my story.

It came time for my parents to go to parent-teacher conferences, and they found out how accommodating the teachers and staff at Rushville High School were being with me. It was everyone's goal to just see me have the best care that I could have. The teachers all knew how serious this was, and I was determined to do whatever it took for me to be okay.

During those frequent trips to Denver, my mom would often ask friends from our church to go with us to be an extra driver for her and to keep her company, as I was often very sick during those times. On one trip, Kathy Dohse went with us. I had an appointment with Dr. Cullen on February 5, and was given more chemotherapy. I had to have a blood transfusion as my counts were so low. I began to itch shortly after they started the transfusion, and luckily my mom was right beside me (as she always was). She noticed that I began to scratch and asked what was wrong. She went to find a nurse, and when she came back, my lips were swollen and I was having a hard time swallowing. The nurse quickly got the doctor and they immediately took me to the emergency room and admitted me to the hospital. It turned out that I was having an allergic reaction to the donor's blood. They put me on mega doses of Benadryl to reduce the swelling. It was a very scary ordeal, especially for my mom to see it all happening right in front of her eyes. I was told later that I could have died from that experience!

Blood transfusions were common during my chemo treatments. Sometimes my blood counts were so low that I would have to have some new blood. We were extra cautious after the allergic reaction, and I never had any problems with transfusions after that. When I would have my chemo treatments, sometimes they would last up to eight hours at a time. I usually watched a movie or played video games or even slept. I did what I could to not think about what was happening to me. It was my way of pretending that this was not real.

One thing that was a huge blessing to us was the love and support of the Church of God friends, such as Gerry Powell, Jan Barrnett, Mary Young, and Karen Shetler. They all took turns going with my mom to my appointments to Denver to help her drive. My Aunt Kathy also helped with the driving on one our many trips. During our travels to Denver and Scottsbluff, the weather did not always cooperate with us. I remembered Mom having to cancel or postpone some of my doctor's appointments due to harsh weather conditions. I can remember one time that we were supposed to be in Denver and we got as far as Kimball, Nebraska, and we ended up staying at a hotel for the night because the weather was too bad to go farther.

On March 14, I had a spinal tap done at the CHOA clinic. We drove home after that and arrived around 6:00 p.m. This was a night I will never forget! That night, Ron Brown, the receivers coach for the Husker football team, came to my house to see me. He was one of Nebraska's best-known assistant coaches, and was touring Western Nebraska promoting his newest Christian book about sports and Christ. He was going to be speaking in our area. It turned out the night that he was scheduled to speak, Mom and I were going to be in Denver for a chemotherapy treatment, so Barb Schaer made special arrangements and told Ron Brown about me. He wanted to meet me at my house, talk with me, and pray with me! Wow, I couldn't believe that he would take time out of his busy schedule to come see me! He showed up late that night after he had done his presentation and surprised me. Barb had told my mom, but she wanted it to be a surprise. To say the least, it was a shocker, but I loved every moment of it! Ron Brown is a very inspirational guy and I admire him a lot. He sat with me, in my own living room, and prayed with me. He told me to never give up and to rely on God to help me through it all.

Receiver coach Ron Brown and I after a Husker game

Ron later made arrangements for my family and I to go to the Nebraska vs. Colorado game in late November, during Thanksgiving weekend. The tickets he gave me were right behind the south goal post, about five rows up. He also made arrangements for me to go into the locker room after the game and meet as well as get autographs from some of the Nebraska players. Nebraska nearly lost that game but won on a last-moment scoring drive that led to a game-winning field goal. Nebraska won the game 34-32. I have been going to Nebraska football games ever since 1993, and as of this writing, I have not missed a season! I have been going to at least one game a year. So being able to go to a Husker game, even when I was sick with cancer, meant the world to me.

On March 19, after talking to both Pastor Harlen Wheeler and our youth pastor, I decided to turn my life over to God. Our whole family got baptized at the Church of God in a special service that day. This will always be a day I won't forget.

For my next doctor's appointment, my mom and I took Gail Glassgow with us. A very bad storm was predicted, but we made it okay. After having my appointment with Dr. Cullen and a treatment, he said I was in remission! My mom and I were so thrilled. But I still had to take several pills. My mom was always on top of that. She would have my pills ready each day, tell me when to take them, and always make sure things were done right. Looking back on that, I don't know how she kept it straight with everything else she was dealing with.

On April 4, I had a spinal tap done at Dr. Cullen's office at the CHOA clinic and had a rare and bad reaction to it. It gave me a very bad backache, and I was up all night! The pain lasted for a week or so. Dr. Packard told me to take some pain medication and I would be fine. My mom stayed home with me to make sure I was okay. By April 10, I was feeling pretty good. I even went to school and worked at Ryan's Market. I was starting to feel as good as you could, being through chemo treatments and spinal taps and everything else I was going through. Those days, in mid to late April, were good days for me.

Then, the first curveball came on April 26. I decided to tell my mom about a lump that I had discovered on my testicle. I was scared to tell anyone about it at first but decided I had better let my parents know. My mom called the doctor and made arrangements for me to be seen as soon as possible. Soon after that, both of my parents and I left for a trip to Denver to see Dr. Cullen. I had an ultrasound done and they discovered a mass on my left testicle.

The operation was set for May 10. I had surgery done with Dr. Chang and he removed my left testicle, and after that, they did more testing. It was confirmed that it was malignant and I had germ cell tumor testicular cancer. Dr. Chang said it was a different type of cancer and was unrelated to the lymphoma. This was pretty shocking news. It was only four months ago I was diagnosed with lymphoma and now another type of cancer. I asked myself, *Can I really handle this?* This type of cancer required surgery right away and lots of aggressive new forms of chemotherapy. They started the chemo after they had performed surgery on me. A few days later, the doctor told us that he had never seen these types of cancer together. They were unrelated. It was also said that I made medical history in Denver because of the two cancers going on at the same time. This called for a powerful type of chemotherapy that required me to spend even more time in Denver. Also, the aggressive type of chemotherapy made me very sick and I was not able to keep any food down. I had four days in a row of potent chemotherapy and was very sick through all of it. The doctors decided to treat my second cancer very intrusively and put the first cancer treatment on hold; then they would pick up again with my lymphoma treatment later.

When I was diagnosed with testicular cancer, I learned that this was the same form of cancer that sidelined famous cyclist Lance Armstrong from competing professionally. After Armstrong was able to overcome his battle with cancer, he went on to win the Tour DeFrance multiple times. I started wearing the yellow Livestrong bracelet after I was diagnosed. Lance Armstrong became an inspiration to me.

My mom was once again devastated, along with the rest of my family, at the news of another cancer, and it being malignant too. We were not getting any good news, and just a few weeks ago I was doing pretty well. None of us could understand what was going on. The next day, I felt pretty good, considering what I had just gone through but was just a little sore.

By then, the doctors had me taking the maximum amount of Prednisone. Some of the side effects are pain in the joints. In my case, it was the Prednisone that caused my pain, possibly because my bones were still growing.

Later in May, my family and I were in Chadron, Nebraska. We went past this old muscle car that had a "For Sale" sign on it. It turned out to be a red 1967 Mustang Fastback. I was very attracted to this car and wanted to take a closer look. Scott Pearson was the owner. He knew a lot about Mustangs, and I later found out he worked on and rebuilt them. He and my mom started to talk while my dad and I looked the car over. While my mom and Scott were talking, somehow it came up that we had been traveling to Denver a lot for medical reasons. Scott told my mom that his family went to Denver for medical treatments too. This caught my mom by surprise, so she asked for a little more information. Well it turned out that their youngest child, their son Jeffrey, had cancer. Jeffrey was only two years old. We found out that both Jeffrey and I went to the same CHOA clinic for our cancer treatments. It was so hard to believe that just because we stopped to look at a Mustang, we met a family who dealt with the same thing as we were currently dealing with, going to the same Childhood Hematology Oncology Associates, and even dealing with the same doctors that we were! This was more than just a coincidence to us! So, the more Scott and my mom talked, the more we found out we had a lot in common. Then Scott's wife, Kris, joined us, and we met their daughter, Jordan, too. So I ended up buying the Mustang from Scott and Kris Pearson, and our families became friends! I still have my Mustang I bought from Scott that day. With the money I was making from the *Omaha World Herald* paper route, I had saved enough to buy new rims for the car. Our great friends Joe and Jerene took me to a place called Colorado Mustang. I was like a kid in a candy store, because everywhere you looked, there were things that you could buy to customize your Mustang. Through the many months I had to be in Denver, Joe and Jerene were nice enough to take me there. Joe himself had a Mustang and we shared our love of the cars together. He even helped me look for and get parts for mine.

Me with my Mustang at the Rushville Car Show

We were soon on the road again, going to yet another doctor's appointment in Denver. On May 31, I started my new phase of treatment. My blood counts were good. Dr. Cullen's wife, Patsy, did another spinal tap, and it went okay, so Dr. Cullen started me on the red chemo again. I did well at first but then got very sick later in the day. On the way home, our van broke down in Ft. Morgan, Colorado. My mom and I had to find a motel to stay in. I was very sick and it was Memorial Day Weekend. The motels were full, but Mom was able to find the last available room, which a more expensive suite with a king-sized bed and a lot of extra room that we didn't need, but we took it anyway. I was too sick to care, and she was just exhausted and frustrated about having van problems. This was just one example of my mom doing whatever it took to make sure I was okay. The van breaking down must have just added to the stress that she was already facing but she always tried to keep a positive attitude through everything.

Later the next day, we got our van fixed. She found out it was the fuel pump. We made it back as far as Minatare and stayed there. We often stayed with my Aunt Louise and my Uncle Martin Atkinson, who lived there. This town was just seven miles from Scottsbluff. This served as a checkpoint for Mom and me. Many times before a trip to Denver, we would go sleep there so we would be about two hours closer, and when I had doctor's appointments in Scottsbluff, it served us well.

Mom and I went to my appointment at the Scottsbluff hospital. This time the form of chemo called for a shot in the leg. Dr. Packard even told us that he had never seen this kind of situation, two cancers at once! That was not very encouraging news to me and even harder for Mom to deal with.

On June 8, Mom and I spent the night in Minatare and headed out to Denver the next day for my red chemo and another shot in the leg. It went well and my counts were good. It was very important to know what my blood counts were during this time because it could mean I may need another blood transfusion.

Later that week, on June 13, I was able to go to a Colorado Rockies game. Mom and I went with Joe and Jerene and had a good time. With Joe and Jerene in Denver, I had the chance, when I felt good, to go to many interesting and fun places there.

Enjoying a Rockies game with my special friends Joe & Jerene

Dr. Cullen even gave me some Colorado Rockies tickets. I was able to see several Rockies games during my doctor's visits. I was also lucky enough to see a Denver Nuggets basketball game too. Later, my Uncle Mike took me to see the rock band Aerosmith. With all of these cancer treatments, which obviously were not fun, there were small perks to having cancer. An example was the Make-A-Wish foundation. That was a big perk. Also, there was an organization in Denver called the Diane Price Fish Foundation. It was that foundation that got us free tickets to the Aerosmith concert and the Nuggets game. I was also given coupons for free dinners to this fancy restaurant and game area called Dave & Busters. They gave me free movie tickets to a nearby movie theater. I must have seen the first Spider-Man movie four times.

On June 14, I felt well enough and had time between treatments, so my mom and I went to the Denver Zoo. I started to have pain in my left side. During the next few weeks, I stayed in Denver in between Park Manor and the hospital. The doctors continued with my chemo treatments. I told Dr. Cullen about the pain in my left side. He ordered X-rays, an ultrasound, and a CAT scan. He put me in the hospital as the pain was so severe. He suspected problems with my pancreas. Dr. Chang said no surgery was needed. All tests done that day showed nothing wrong. Dr. Cullen thought it must have been just an infection.

Morey and Dorothy Bruce, friends from church, brought my dad and Kristin to Denver that weekend. Kristin had fallen while rollerblading while she was baby-sitting. She had a terrible case of road rash. She almost got put in the hospital. It was so bad, she ended up in the ER in Denver! It was real hard on Mom to have both Kristin and I with medical problems! Later that week, I started feeling somewhat better. I ate pretty well and was able to walk around some. Dr. Cullen told us it could be possible pancreatitis, my spleen, blocked arteries, or dead or enlarged lymph nodes in the groin. He said he didn't think it had anything to do with my lymphoma. He said I was still in remission! While on chemo, there is a chance of other body parts getting harmed because of the poisonous chemo drugs.

Joe and Jerene came to visit a few days later. I had another CAT scan done to see if they could figure out what was going on and why this happened. It showed three large nodes in the abdomen, but they were still deciding what to do. The pain got much better, and my mom and I ordered pizza and watched movies in my room. It was a way to escape and stop thinking about what was happening to me, and a chance for Mom to update them on how I was feeling.

The doctors and surgeons decided to do surgery to see what the cluster of dead lymph nodes was. Joe and Jerene came again to be with my mom and keep her company during the long surgery. I made it through but the surgeon was not optimistic at all and thought it could be bad news.

Dr. Cullen called later that day and said it was malignant germ cell cancer and that I would have to wait for the surgery to heal before he gave me any more chemo. One of my favorite aunts came to visit me shortly after that. I can remember Aunt Trish and me blowing bubbles with our gum together and seeing who could get the biggest bubble. I enjoyed my time with her. She stayed with me for a few days and was good company for my mom.

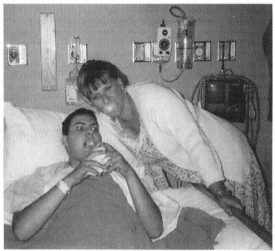

Bubble gum blowing contest with Aunt Trish

After my surgery, I had Randy and Cathy Atkinson and Aunt Trish as visitors. I was pretty sore. It was a huge relief to get the tube taken out of my nose! I even went for a very short walk, was able to take a shower, and slept pretty well that night.

After my surgery, I was finally getting hungry but all the nurses would allow me was a couple of popsicles! Pretty sad when *that* was the highlight of my day! My dad and Kristin went to the Denver Zoo, and Aunt Trish and my mom visited. Later that week, Aunt Trish took Kristin back as far as North

Platte, and then Jerry and Sue Scott picked her up there and took her home.

On June 26, I had a chest X-ray and hearing test done as the doctor said the chemo could affect my hearing. The surgeon said I was doing fine, so I was dismissed from the hospital. We had a conference with Dr. Cullen and my parents to plan for a new treatment protocol. They planned to attack the germ cell cancer with full force for four months and then pick back up with the lymphoma plan. Dr. Cullen said the cure rate was 85-90 percent.

My mom and I stayed at Park Manor during my next phase of chemotherapy treatments. The CHOA clinic was across the street from Park Manor, so it was easy for Mom and me to get there. My first dose of the new chemotherapy treatment plan was for eight hours.

Presbyterian St. Luke's Hospital in Denver where I was a patient most of the time

My mom and I would walk over, and I would be in a small room with a bed and TV and would get hooked up to an IV through which the chemo was given. Eight hours was a long time. I could watch all the movies I wanted, play video games, or even sleep. This particular form of chemo left a metal taste in my mouth. I would drink a lot to get rid of that taste. This situation was probably equally hard on my mom. Having to watch her only son being hooked up to IVs and do nothing but sit there watching. Later that week, my dad went home on the Denver Coach. He really tried to keep as steady a work schedule as he could. His job did not allow him nearly as much time off as my Mom was able to take. Soon after that, we met with Dr. Cullen. He said the chest X-ray looked a lot better and I would get to go home really soon. I was in Denver for almost the whole month of June.

During the week of the Fourth of July, Rushville was hosting an all-class reunion. They had a parade and lots of activities going on in town. It was really hot and I did not feel well, so I had to come home right after the parade. I wanted to stay out and see all my friends, but I just was not feeling up to it. I was being bothered with hip pain as well. The next day, I felt better and went to church and invited several friends to our house for ice cream sundaes after the fireworks. We had a good turnout and a enjoyed visiting with everyone.

The next week, Mom and I were in Scottsbluff again for blood counts. Dr. Packard said I was doing well. Then it came time for us to take another trip to Denver for more chemo. This next dose was for four straight days of eight-hour treatments. I was not looking forward to any of it! I had a spinal tap and chest X-ray done also. After all of that, I did get pretty sick. Joe and Jerene visited again.

During this phase of chemo, I met another kid, age sixteen, from Denver who also had testicular cancer. That day we played video games together. By the fourth straight day of eight long hours of chemo, I started to feel pretty nauseous, but I made it through the best I could.

On the way home toward the end of July, the air conditioner went out on our van. It was 103 degrees out and I was feeling sick.

When I was back in Rushville, I was able to work at Ryan's Market. Ryan Lovell, the owner, would let me work there whenever I could. Later on in late summer, my dad and I were able to go to a concert in Valentine and then to a Big Foot show the next day. It was nice that I was well enough to do some things with my dad.

On August 7, Mom and I left for Denver again. We went to Scottsbluff on our way to get my blood count done first; the counts were good. Our youth pastor drove to Denver and was going to take me to the Rockies game the next day. But, on the way to Denver, our van decided to quit on us in the middle of a busy street. The van had vapor locked! My mom and the youth pastor were able to push it off the side of the road. I was well enough to go to the Rockies game the next day. We had incredible seats, right behind home plate!

The next day, I had a chemo treatment. It went as well as it could. During all this time getting chemo, I would see a lot of the same nurses. One of my favorites was Lisa Higgins, a nurse on the pediatric floor of the hospital. She was very nice and good-looking too, and treated my mom really well. She even told my mom about the Make-A-Wish program and said that I would be a good candidate to make a wish.

Me and Lisa who was my favorite nurse at the hospital

I had a lot of visitors come to Denver during this time. Once, Aunt Sharon and Jamie stopped to visit me. They stayed for a while and visited with my mom as well. It was a nice visit.

When Mom and I left to come home, I was sick the whole way home. Of all things to go wrong, the van quit us again in Alliance. It vapor locked once more. It was 110 degrees out! It was not a good day for either Mom or me. She was frustrated; I was sick; and we were stranded!

The next week was fair week in Gordon, and school was right around the corner. I had started limping noticeably about two weeks before and told Dr. Cullen about the pain in my hip, but he said it was probably a pulled muscle. This proved to be wrong and he did not know what was happening to me.

Soon after that, I worked once more at Ryan's Market but had to quit because it just was not in my best interest to continue working there with cancer and my hips hurting me. Everyone at the store completely understood and wished me the best.

On August 18, my mom and I went to Scottsbluff to get my blood work checked. The test came back okay. I told Dr. Packard about my hips hurting really badly. He ordered a bone scan of my left hip.

I then started my first day of my senior year at Rushville High School. I remember walking down the halls, going to class, and falling flat on the first floor. My hip just gave out on me and I was in severe pain. The pain was so bad, I could not even stand back up to walk. My mom was called to the school and I was taken home. We called Dr. Packard. He told us the bone scan showed deterioration of bone caused by the steroids. He then referred me to the orthopedic surgeon.

The pain in my hip was getting so bad that I could hardly walk. I went to school for a half day the next day. Mom and I made a trip to Gordon and got crutches to help me walk. I woke up in the night with bad back and head pain. Mom took me to the ER in Scottsbluff. While there, I went to see the orthopedic surgeon. He ordered more tests. He did not think it was cancer but wanted to do an MRI. The results of the MRI would not be ready until Monday. I got my counts done in Scottsbluff and was told it was okay to come to Denver for treatment later on that week. Jerry and Sue Scott loaned us their van to go to Denver because of the many problems we were having with our van.

I got to know the orthopedic surgeon, Dr. Cynthia Kelly. She took a look at my case and my cancer and determined I had avascular necrosis. This is the same condition that ended pro football and baseball player Bo Jackson's career. Dr. Kelly told me that there were signs of avasular necrosis in both of my hips caused by the high doses of Prednisone taken. My left hip was more severe. She told me that my left hip had already collapsed and that was why I was in so much pain. My right hip showed extensive damage as well. She wanted to do surgery to repair the left hip.

Me and my Orthopedic Surgeon Dr. Cynthia Kelly

The surgery was scheduled for September 20. Dr. Kelly wanted to wait and do surgery on my right hip after I graduated from high school. She told me that my knees were both damaged as well and would need surgery in the near future. This was all caused by taking the massive amounts of Prednisone. The doctors told me if I had not had the massive amounts of Prednisone, I would not have survived the cancer. Sometimes I wish I could have taken a chance on that, as the hip and knee problems completely changed my life and limit me to this day as to what I can and cannot do.

Before the hip surgery, the doctors discovered a mass in my stomach area. This was from the lymphoma. The cancer had spread from my neck area to my stomach. So the doctors and surgeons told my family and me that they were going to do surgery on my left hip and also take the cancerous mass out of my stomach at the same time! This surgery could take up to ten hours. The team of doctors told us that this would be the best way to do it and that it needed to be done right away. At this point, I did not think anything could get any worse, but I was wrong!

It was time once again for my four-day chemo treatment. On the way to Denver, we stopped in Scottsbluff to pick up the X-rays and take them with us to Denver. We got to Denver just before a terrible hail storm hit. We went through a real hard downpour. It was hard for Mom to even see to drive. It was kind of a scary trip, and for once, it was a relief to be in Denver!

The next day, I had my first round of germ cell chemo. I was very sick but slept most of the day. Dr. Cullen wanted to consult with Dr. Kelly to decide how they were going to do the surgery for sure. That night, Joe and Jerene brought supper to my room.

On my second day of chemo, I was feeling pretty sick. They had me doped up on pain medication most of the day. Mom took me for a wheelchair ride and we went to see my favorite nurse, Lisa, again. On the third day, I felt sick most of the day and slept a lot. Dr. Kelly came to see me. She told my mom and me that she wanted to do a cement-type surgery on me in a few weeks. She said I would have to recuperate from my chemo first.

Finally, it was the last day of treatment. Mom and I left to come home from Denver. I felt sick the whole trip. On the way, we stopped to see Dr. Freidline, who was the orthopedic surgeon in Scottsbluff. He told us the same thing that Dr. Kelly told us in Denver, that I would need surgery soon.

Soon after that, it was Rushville Fun Days. I felt somewhat better, so I decided to drive my Mustang in the parade. I put my car in the car show and got second place. I was pretty well worn out but made it through the day, but only with the help of crutches. That night, Mom and Dad had me start sleeping in their room so I would not have to use the stairs, as my hip was bothering me so much. Even when we were at home, my mom was still my special nurse. She took such good care of me and never really rested because I was so sick.

When I was able, I went to school. I had to have the help of crutches just to get around. All the teachers were so understanding and helpful. I can remember them letting me leave class early to go use the elevator so I could be the first in line at lunch.

Our family was still having some major van problems. Then on September 7, we got an amazing gift. It turned out that our Church of God family was taking love offerings for us. My senior classmates had a fundraiser as well. The money all together totaled $1600, and some great friends of ours chipped in with another $1000 to my parents, so they were able to get another van.

Our friends Joe and Jerene contacted the *Omaha World Herald* and let them know of our situation. They in return were touched by our story and printed an article about our family's vehicle problems and concerns. Because of the generosity of complete strangers, my parents were able to pay off the remaining balance of the van. They were amazed and completely humbled by the kindness of these people. My mom would now have a new van to take me to my doctor's appointments. The following is the actual article from September 20, 2000:

Van Problems Get in the Way

The temperature was a hundred-something degrees, the air conditioning wasn't working and now the van wouldn't start. Diane Moore was the first one at the stoplight, and the line of cars behind her started honking. But her mind wasn't on the van or the other cars. She was worried about her 17-year-old son, Brad. He has just been through three eight-hour days of chemotherapy, and the heat was getting to him. They couldn't be stuck in the July sun, not today.

The Moore family tried to ignore the little things-car problems, medical bills-since Brad was diagnosed with cancer on New Year's Day. Their focus is on Brad and getting him better. But sometimes the little things get in the way, like they did this July in Alliance, Neb., on the way home from Brad's treatment in Denver. A kind stranger helped Diane move her car out of the street that day, and she took Brad into an air-conditioned store while the van cooled down. It was the second time the van had stranded them between Denver and their home in Rushville, Neb. The first time was on Memorial Day weekend in Fort Morgan, Colo. The fuel pump gave out, and Diane and Brad were lucky to get the last available room at the Comfort Inn. Now, Diane borrows a friend's van for the semi-monthly trips to Denver. The Moores need to do something about their own vehicle-pay for another expensive repair or trade it for something more reliable-but both options call for money they can't spare right now.

Everything Changed

As Diane and her husband, Lee, drove Brad to Denver
this week's slate of appointments and tests, they talked
about how much had changed in their lives since January.
They used to worry about money and their jobs and
their house. "Those things don't seem important now
at all," Diane said. When Brad was diagnosed with
non-Hodgkin's lymphoma, I wrote an article about the
great lengths he went to keep his World-Herald paper
route. On days when he couldn't make it, his family helped
out, and his classmates at Rushville High took on the
route for three weeks. Brad still has the paper route. "He's
got determination," his mother said, "and doesn't want
to give up . . ." We feel blessed to have a great kid with
an attitude like that. It's helped us get through it" Brad
kept the paper route and his other job, sacking groceries,
even after he was diagnosed with a second type of cancer,
germ-cell. His doctors say the two cancers are unrelated.
"It's been a real scare to us," Diane said, "to see the
doctors shaking their heads," not sure what
is wrong with Brad.

So Generous

The cancer treatment has caused further problems.
Brad's hipbones are deteriorating. He finally had to give up
his job at the grocery store when he started needing crutches
to walk. If all goes well, Brad might have hip surgery
this week. Through everything, the people in Rushville
and nearby Gordon have stood by the Moores. Diane's
co-workers at the Sheridan County Courthouse and Lee's
at the Farmers Co-op have been understanding, letting

them take time off when they need to be with Brad. Their congregation at the Church of God in Gordon has helped, too, and the high school kids held a bakeless bake sale. The community even threw a big fund-raiser and set up a bank account for donations-the Brad Moore Fund, First National Bank of Gordon, Box 290, Gordon, Neb., 69343. "It's been overwhelming how nice people have been," Diane said, "how supportive." The Moore family has had trouble accepting so much generosity. It's hard for Diane even to talk about their situation, especially to a reporter. She doesn't want any undue attention. Everyone already has helped so much. "I would just trade everything . . ." she said, "for my son to be healthy. I don't want money or a different vehicle or anything. "I just want him to be OK."

I was scheduled to have surgery on my left hip on September 20, the day the article was written. Kristin stayed with Grandma and Grandpa Cerny. Mom and Dad and I left for Denver again. We stayed the night in Scottsbluff. When I got to Denver, I had more CAT scans done. The doctors found an enlarged lymph node in my abdomen near my kidney. The doctors teamed up to decide how they would operate on that.

The night before surgery, my parents and I had a consultation with Dr. Cullen and Dr. Kelly. They decided it was best to do stomach surgery first and then flip me over and do the left hip surgery. They predicted it to be about a seven to ten hour surgery, which turned out to be pretty accurate! This was not too exciting for me to think about, but I tried to think of it as a big sleep and not to worry. Though this was not easy for my mom to do! She was taking things pretty hard.

The night before my surgery, Randy and Cathy Atkinson took my parents and me out to the Hard Rock Café for supper.

It was a good way for all of us to relax. I was able to eat a nice meal, but I had to prepare for the big surgery the next day.

September 20, I had surgery for removal of the enlarged node in my abdomen and then hip surgery to cap off the left hip bone. Pastor Harlen and Matt Wheeler came to see me, and of course Joe and Jerene were there to support us. I made it through both surgeries, doing as good as could be expected.

The next day I was feeling really sore. I had my stomach cut open again and my left hip bone capped off. I was doped up pretty well. The nurses were in my room twice that day and had me get out of bed and stand. Mom wanted to just slap them and tell them to leave me alone. I was hooked up to so many tubes and wires; it took a team to help me even sit up! Wow! I was so sore! I felt the itchies from all the drugs I was on. I even managed to pull out the tube in my nose that was pumping bile out of my stomach. I wasn't supposed to do that! I did this in my sleep. I was then in trouble with the nurses!

While in the hospital the next night, I was able to have the catheter taken out, but not soon enough for me! What a relief! They had me on a morphine pump so I could push it when I felt I needed more pain control. I did a lot of sleeping. I was told I said some pretty off-the-wall things. I guess the drugs made me do that.

Shortly after my big surgery, my cousin Jodi got married, but I was in Denver. Kristin was the only one in our family who was able to attend the wedding.

The next day, I got up once and took a few steps. I had to have two units of blood that day. I managed to watch some of the Nebraska football game that was on TV. That was the highlight of my day. I kept dozing off so I missed quite a bit of it.

The next couple of days, I started to feel somewhat better and got to walk more. Dr. Kelly came in to see me and said I was doing pretty well. Dad decided to stay with Mom and me and drive home with us.

I was finally released from the hospital. We had the nurses help my parents get me loaded in the van. That was quite an ordeal, and I was so sore in both my stomach and hip area. I got wedged into the van with a lot of pillows and props! I took up the entire back of the van. I don't remember much of the trip home as I was pretty well drugged up; I slept most of the way.

Only ten days after my major surgeries, my family and I left to go to Lincoln for a Husker game. On the way to Lincoln, we stayed in Tilden with the Linse family. I was given four tickets from the Make-A-Wish foundation to attend the Nebraska-Missouri game on September 30. Saturdays in Nebraska were considered Husker game day. This was really soon after I had major surgery! I truly had no business being there. I was very determined to go to this game. In fact, it really scared my mom to take me to this game as she thought it was much too soon for me to be out and about. I had actually had double surgery since they did surgery on my hip and removed the malignant mass in my stomach they also found. I was on crutches and there were fresh stitches in my stomach and left hip. I was even thinking to myself that I probably should not have been there.

It was much too soon after surgery to be at a football game.

I went in a wheelchair and got to meet Ron Brown after the game. I had seats in the second row! We stayed with our friends, the Boyers. I have to say it was one of the best moments of my life! One of the memories my mom had about that game was watching me and seeing how happy I was that I got to be there. She was so proud of my strength and courage throughout this cancer experience. She remembers the national anthem being sung before the game and looking over at me and seeing me cry. I was not crying because of pain but because of happiness! In spite of all the hard times, with all my cancer treatments and traveling for chemotherapy, I still managed to get to go to a Nebraska Husker game. Nebraska ended up beating Missouri 42-24. It was a true dream for me and the highlight of a very tough time in my life. I will always remember that moment, that game, and having the feeling of remembering what all I had overcome so far in my life! Everyone was so proud of my courage and determination. I was mentally tough and would never have told Mom that I was in pain. I wanted to be there so bad that I would have gone either way. The next day, we stopped in Grand Island on the way home to see Aunt Trish and family.

Me with Herbie Husker at a Nebraska Football game

When I got back to Rushville, it was homecoming week at RHS. I managed to recuperate from the surgeries pretty well and started at school as soon as I could, back on crutches. I got along as good as could be expected I was able to go all day some days; other days I couldn't. I went to school the whole week of homecoming and was lucky to not have a doctor's appointment. Friday came, and I went to the homecoming pep rally. I was able to attend the Gordon vs. Rushville football game. I was feeling pretty good that night, although I did have to hobble around on my crutches. My classmates honored me by making me the team captain of the football team. I even went to the homecoming dance and danced without crutches.

Kristin & I at Rushville Homecoming 2000

Later in October, during parent-teacher conferences that semester, my favorite teacher, Mr. Urbach, came over to my house afterward to visit. I gave him a puzzle of the Civil War that I had put together in my free time. It was way one thousand pieces. He was as much into the Civil War as I was. That same night, he even presented me with a runner-up medal that Rushville earned in state wresting. Since I was the team manager, he thought that I deserved a medal as well.

Soon, Mom and I left for my next doctor's appointment in Denver, but only made it as far as Kimball and then stayed the night there. The trips were getting harder and harder for Mom to deal with. It was a long drive for her, and I was never much help. While in Denver, I got my normal spinal tap and chemo done. I also saw Dr. Kelly on this visit. She looked me over and told me to put the crutches away and said I was healing really well.

When I got back to Rushville, I went to school without crutches but overdid it, so I went back on crutches the next day. I started working with Robin Stewart, a physical therapist who came to work with me at school as well as occasionally at home.

The next trip to Denver, Mom and I left after school but only went as far as Minatare. Once we were in Denver again, I had an appointment with Dr. Cullen and had a spinal tap and a chemo shot of ARA-C.

That next Friday night, I was honored again. Since the football team had named me captain, I got to go on the field for the coin toss. It was also parent night, so both Mom and Dad walked out with me during halftime.

The next week, Jerry and Sue Scott had Mom and me over for dinner and let me use their hot tub to help my hips. Dr. Kelly recommended that I use a hot tub to do exercises so that it would not put pressure on my hips. She encouraged my family to get one for home use.

The following week, I was finally able to do the paper route again. My mom helped me each morning. I continued to work with Robin Stewart for physical therapy, and I also used the hot tub when I was able too.

By November, I started to have pain in my right hip. I was also having muscle pain and spasms in my left hip. When I told Dr. Kelly about the pain I was having in my right hip, she told me I would have to wait a while before I would be ready for surgery again.

The next doctor's appointment came soon, and the weather was expected to be snowy. Dad was able to take off work and go with Mom and me to Denver. I checked into the hospital early the next morning and had scans done. Dr. Cullen said the scan showed something on my lungs. He ordered a CAT scan, but it was not determined that anything else was wrong at that time. Dr. Cullen told me that I was officially on maintenance therapy now. I would take oral doses of chemo for the next month. I had to start taking sixteen methotrexate pills every day. I was able to go to school during that time but I was still having bad pain in both of my hips, so I started using crutches again.

Thanksgiving was just around the corner, and Husker Coach, Ron Brown, made arrangements for our family to go to this game and go into the locker room afterward. Was I ever excited for this game on November 23!

My family left early the next morning for Lincoln to go to the game. We met up with Mr. Squier, my high school superintendant, before the game. Chuck was also on the chain gang for the Big 12 Conference at Nebraska home games. It was such an exciting game! Nebraska won! I was able to meet up with Ron Brown after the game, and he took me to the locker room, where my dad and I got to meet some of the players. We met up with John and Mel Strasburger, some great friends of our family. We later went out to dinner with them.

I can remember this game so well! Nebraska nearly lost. Colorado went ahead of Nebraska late in the fourth quarter and went for a two-point conversion and made it. That made the score 32-31, with Colorado winning. There was less than a minute left in the football game. Nebraska's quarterback, Eric Crouch, passed down field to get the Huskers into field goal position, and Josh Brown kicked a 29-yard game-winning field goal as time expired. To see that live was probably the most excited I had ever been. I remember telling my mom that if Nebraska lost, no players would want to meet me. I would have no chance at getting any autographs.

My family and I at the Husker game with Chuck Squier

The next day, my family stayed in Lincoln. We met up with Gary and Mary Boyer for breakfast, and Gary took my dad and me on a tour of the state capitol, while Mary took my mom and Kristin shopping. He was able to give us private tour of the capitol building.

On December 7, I got up and did the paper route by myself, came home, ate breakfast, and went to school. It was our plan that I would go to school until noon, Mom would work in the morning, and then we would leave for my appointment, but I came home about ten o'clock feeling really sick. I was having very bad stomach pain. My mom came home and found me on the floor, holding my stomach, and nearly crying because I was in so much pain. We were supposed to leave for Denver for a chemotherapy treatment by noon that day. My mom loaded me in the van, we got as far as Scottsbluff, and my stomach hurt so bad that we had to go to the Emergency Room at the Scottsbluff Hospital. Dr. Packard immediately put me in the hospital. He was not sure what was wrong with me. They did more tests and could not find anything wrong. He did not think it had anything to do with more cancer. I got sick seven times that night. I had a very rough night and was extremely ill. They finally injected some dye into me and discovered a blockage in my bowels. The surgeons determined that I was in so much pain because of an abdominal bowel obstruction. The surgeon then performed emergency surgery for the bowel obstruction. We were later told that it was caused by the scar tissue from the previous surgeries done on my stomach in September. The doctors told us that there was a small tissue in my stomach lining that got twisted. They even said the tissue was as small as a piano wire and somehow wrapped around my bowels. This was a type of pain that is indescribable! Mom said she remembers me just looking really white in the face and that I was very out of it.

There was a lot of talk going around at school about my health and how I was doing. My mom and I later found out that it was said that I did not make it. So the rumor was that I had died. Well my sister heard that and she called Mom and said that students were saying that I had died. What happened was that I was supposed to have an appointment in Denver, but I got that stomach pain and Dr. Packard put me in the hospital and did some tests. So the word got out that I was headed to Denver, but didn't make it. That is how the rumor started that I had died. Rumors can be so bad. This was another thing that made it especially hard on my Mom.

After my third stomach surgery, I pulled out the tube from my nose again. I wish it was just a dream but it was very real. Once again, I was in big trouble with the nurses. They were not happy with me and I had to have it reinserted while I was awake. That really made me wish I had never ever pulled it out in the first place. Dr. Packard came to see me a few days after and said I was doing much better and I would be able to go off the morphine. The next day I was able to get up and walk up and down the hospital halls with the nurse's help, even though my scar on my stomach was bigger than the previous ones and was really sore.

After about a week and a half in the hospital, I was feeling much better, so Dr. Packard said I could go home. Mom stayed home with me the rest of the day. Robin, my therapist, came to the house to work with me. The next day I was able to go back to school and got along fine. I got asked a lot of questions. My friends and teachers wanted to know all about my latest surgery. After school that day, I went to the Rushville clinic and got my staples pulled out of my stomach.

The next week, Mom and I left for Denver for another doctor's appointment. We met up with Joe and Jerene for dinner. After my appointment with Dr. Cullen, Mom and I met with Dr. Kelly. She ordered an MRI on my left knee. She recommended surgery to be done soon, to repair the damage to my knee.

A few days went by and I went to Christmas Eve church services with my family and enjoyed being home. On Christmas day, my whole family went to Grandma and Grandpa Cerny's for our usual Christmas day get-together. My whole family was really happy to see me and was glad I was doing as well as I was.

After Christmas was over, I got another late Christmas gift. The Make-A-Wish foundation was going to grant me my wish of a complete home theater system. Now it was my understanding that the Make-A-Wish foundation only granted wishes to kids that were dying. But that was not true. I was told I could have any one thing. I could go on a trip to Africa if I wanted to, because they told me that was one of the wishes someone asked for once. So I really thought this over and really wanted to go the Nebraska Bowl Game that year and go out on the field. But since I pretty much did that during the Nebraska vs. Colorado game, I decided to do something else. After careful thought, I decided to ask for the biggest big screen TV and all of the surround sound speakers and best equipment I could get. They said no problem. My mom and I met with Theresa Hopping from Scottsbluff, and she took me to Video Kingdom in Scottsbluff. While I was there, I just pointed out what I wanted and got it. I was told that the sky was the limit, so I picked what I thought was the best equipment. On December 27, my wish was granted; I got a complete home theatre system from the Make-A-Wish foundation.

Me with my "Make-A-Wish" gift

Two guys from Video Kingdom came to my house in Rushville and unloaded a fifty-five-inch TV. Those guys had trouble unloading the TV. It would not even fit in the basement. They had to cut a hole in the roof in the basement to make it fit. It took them almost seven hours to bring everything down to the basement and hook it up. These two guys were so nice, and they showed me how to make everything work. They also said that the TV "goes with the house" because it was such a tight fit getting down the stairs. They thought we would never be able to get it back out! But with the recent advances in technology, especially big screen TVs, I ended up selling that TV. I used the money to buy another soon after that. I had that TV for seven years and really enjoyed it. I did keep the surround sound speakers and all the other stuff that came with it. I am so thankful I was able to have the chance to make a wish like that.

New Years was quickly coming up. My family and I survived the first year of me having cancer. I overcame a lot within that first year, with many surgeries and chemotherapy treatments. I hoped that it would all just go away and I could get on with the rest of my life and put this whole experience behind me. It did not work out that way. By this time, Mom and I could pretty well tell you every crack and every pothole in the road between home and the Denver Rocky Mountain Cancer Clinic. The year 2000 was the worst year for me, but 2001 looked to be no piece of cake either.

Chapter 3

Graduating with My Class of 2001

The year 2001 would be just about as busy a year for me as 2000 was. In mid-January, my mom and I were scheduled for an appointment in Scottsbluff to meet with Dr. Packard. I was given my first dose of chemo in the year 2001.

Soon it was Super Bowl Sunday. We had the Wheelers and Strasburgers over to watch the game, and Mom fixed everyone dinner. The Ravens beat the Giants 34-7. Later the next month, my dad and I were given tickets for state wrestling in Lincoln. Even though the roads were very icy, we made it. I was really glad I had the chance to go. Rushville won another state title that year. There were several families from Rushville that traveled to Lincoln. Rushville wrestling was favored to win the Class D state title that season, and they did.

In early March, Mom, Dad, Kristin, and I left for Denver. I had an appointment with Dr. Kelly, the orthopedic surgeon. She told me with all the problems in my hips and knees that she could work on me for the next ten weeks and still not be done with me. I guess that was a nice way of saying my legs were a mess! After my appointment, Joe and Jerene met up with us and took us on a tour of the Denver Mint. It was very interesting to see how the money was made. Then we all went to see an IMAX movie, which was really cool.

That was the first time I had ever seen one. My family and I were able to stay at the Renaissance Motel. It was one of the nicest motels I have ever been to. The American Cancer Society helped us with the expenses. The next day, I had an appointment with Dr. Cullen and early scans at the hospital. I then had a spinal tap and chemo treatment at CHOA. Dr. Cullen and the radiologist found three nodes that showed up that looked suspicious to him, but they were not too large. Dr. Cullen told us that he wanted to keep a close eye on those nodes and check in three months for any changes in size.

Later in March, Kristin and I went to a Spring Retreat at Victory Heights Bible Camp. For the first time since being diagnosed, I was away from my mom. I had to take all my medications and flush out my Groshong by myself. It was weird not seeing my mom that night because she and I spent so much time together due to my cancer. She was always there to take care of me. I missed her that night, but I was only gone through the weekend. When I got back, I was able to go to school. I usually drove my Mustang to school. Because of my hip pain and having a hard time walking, I decided to park in the handicapped parking spot at the school since I was running late one day. Well, I got a ticket" from one of the Rushville officers for parking my Mustang in the handicap parking stall. My mom and I were upset with this ticket and embarrassed too because he waited until school was out. Everyone watching and laughing because I got a ticket. The officer was not even on duty. The county attorney decided he would *not* file charges but told me to get a handicap hang tag for my vehicle, because I deserved to have one. I had no problem with getting a doctor to sign the paperwork for me to get a handicap tag. To this day, I hardly ever use it.

Throughout my school days, all of my classmates were really concerned about my health. Some of them would come over to visit too. One thing that my classmates did that I will never forget was taking over the paper route during the time I was gone. I was later told that some of my classmates' parents organized a schedule so my classmates could take turns delivering the *Omaha World Herald.* I was told that history class was their meeting time to discuss which three classmates were going to do it for the week. During that time, the history class was taught by Nate Urbach, who was also head wrestling coach. He was a great guy. To this day, I would say it was one of the nicest things that anyone has ever done for me. I love my classmates from the class of 2001. They are the best friends anyone could ever have.

The school year was moving fast; it was already my senior prom. I remember having a good time with my friends and dancing with no crutches. Later that month I was honored at the RHS Activities Banquet by football coach Kelly Stouffer. I was given a medal as honorary team captain of the RHS football team. Mr. Urbach also gave me an honorable mention as being the manager of the wrestling team. (These awards were very nice and it really showed the character of my school and friends, who truly cared for me and wanted me to get better. You can really thank small towns. They bond with each other and everyone is friends.)

My Mom and I before Prom

Soon after that, my family and I went to the senior supper. I was honored again by my classmates and was presented a plaque by the senior class president, Jesse Clarke. He made a presentation and stated how my classmates all admired my tenacity, and they all wished me good luck. I remember getting tears in my eyes because of all the nice things my classmates were doing for me, and how helpful they were if I ever needed anything.

During the time I spent at home, there would be teachers who would volunteer to come to my house and try to keep me caught up with the rest of the class. Both Mrs. Wellnitz and Mrs. Johnson made some house visits to help with English assignments. That is why I was so lucky to finish high school with my class.

My senior graduation day was set for Mother's Day, May 13. My mom said it was one of the best Mother's Day she ever had. I was able to walk across the stage and get my diploma with the rest of my classmates! I went to church that morning and was honored there too. This was a very proud moment for my parents and a big accomplishment for me! Just thinking of all the stuff that I had been through, it was a milestone for me. I was so happy to be able to graduate from high school with the same class that I had started grade school with. I did not have to get held back because of being gone so often at doctor appointments. I was very happy to graduate with the class of 2001.

My parents and Kristin hosted a graduation reception/party at my house, in the backyard. Once again, we had a very good turnout. It was a really nice day. My legs were hurting pretty bad by the end of the day, but I was on such energy high, knowing that I graduated, that I did not even care. I paid for it the next day though!

Three days after graduation, I was scheduled to have surgery once again, this time on my right hip. Dr. Kelly said it was important and needed to be done. I knew how important it was too, as I was in pain all the time. The surgery went well and she performed the same cement-type surgery as she had done on the left hip. We knew it then that it was only a temporary fix and I would face more surgeries in the future. We just didn't know at that time how long this procedure might last.

That summer was spent recovering from hip surgery and going to physical therapy. I went most every day and did exercises in our hot tub. My family was able to get a hot tub with a lot of help from friends, especially Sue and Jerry Scott. It was a relief to be able to work out and not put stress on my legs.

....

It was on May 16 I checked into the hospital for my right hip surgery and also my knee too. The surgery lasted six hours, and Joe and Jerene came to keep my mom company while I was in surgery. Afterward, Dr. Kelly came in and said I was doing well. Dr. Cullen came to see me too and thought the same. Physical therapy came in to get me out of bed, but I was just too weak to get up. The therapist said she would check back later that afternoon. When she came back, I was able to stand for a short while and take a few steps. After having hip and knee surgery, I pretty much had to learn how to walk again. She had to instruct me on the proper way so I would not hurt myself. It was a really hard surgery to just bounce back from. It took a lot of hard work and a lot of physical therapy. The next couple of days, my appetite came back and I was able to eat some real food. The physical therapist came again the following day and I was able to walk and take even more steps. She was really happy with the progress I was making. After being in the hospital almost two weeks, Dr. Cullen and Dr. Kelly came in and told me that I could go home. That was exciting news for Mom and me! Dr. Kelly stressed that it was really important to keep up with physical therapy.

After I got back home, my mom made arrangements for the home health nurses to come to our home and check on my blood counts since I had to be on blood thinners for a while so I would not develop any blood clots. During the next few days, I went to Gordon and got to know Kim Marlatt really well. She was my physical therapist. I set up regular appointments with her for the whole summer.

On May 30, it was time once again for Mom and me to go to Denver for another checkup. We checked into the hospital early for more scans. Dr. Cullen said I was doing fine. I had a good checkup that trip. I was also seen by Dr. Kelly. She said my hip was healing very well.

In June, I was asked to be a guest speaker at the annual Relay for Life in Chadron. It was a very hot and windy day. There was a good turn out and a lot of our friends from church were there to support me. We even had a team from Church of God, and our team raised the most money for the American Cancer Society. I told my story to the crowd there. And if I knew then what I know now . . . my story was just beginning.

On the Fourth of July, I was able to enjoy time with my family, and I took a drive through the Black Hills. Later that evening Kristin and I went over to Tyler Fisher's (Kristin's boyfriend) for fireworks. Later that month, I started a part-time job working at the vet clinic in Gordon for Dave and Janet Wilson. The job was easy—just answering their phone and taking messages if they were busy. They were friends of our family and knew that I could not do too much. This worked out really well for me as I was in Gordon almost every day anyway because of physical therapy.

For my next doctor's appointment at the end of July, my whole family packed up and we left for Denver. We also took friends Josh Shetler and Amanda Linse with us. We were able to go to another Rockies game and to the IMAX theater with Joe and Jerene, and then out to supper. It was a good time, and I was feeling pretty good. My appointment went well too. Once again, the American Cancer Society helped my family with hotel expenses.

Shortly after, I was back home. The Rushville baseball team won their district and got to go to state baseball in Wakefield for the championship games. I was able to go with Jesse Clarke and his family. Vic, Jesse's dad was the coach of the team. Even though I could no longer play, I tried to support my team members and cheer them on when I could. The team got together and signed a baseball to give me when we all got home.

This is a story printed by the *Chadron Record* on July 24, 2001.

Cancer Survivor Still Recovering from Treatment

Brad Moore lounged on an easy chair by an open window in his house. Part of the day had been spent at his grandmother's house, and now the 18-year-old high school graduate was depleted of energy. "That's what I notice most," his mother, Diane, said. "He doesn't have as much energy as he used to." She's also noticed that her son's hair has come back in a darker shade of brown after the chemo treatments. She noticed that Brad is a survivor. It was Jan. 1 of 2000 when Brad's parents, Diane and Lee, took him to Gordon Memorial Hospital to see why his neck was hurting. He complained because it hurt every time he turned his head. They never guessed it might be cancer. "We were totally shocked. Brad has never been sick in his life," Diane said. (My friends were shocked because I was a healthy, active teen,) Brad said.

"The Disease"

On Jan. 6, 2000, Brad was diagnosed with lymphoblastic lymphoma. Malignant tumors had invaded his neck and chest. Brad was originally sent to Scottsbluff for treatments, but when doctors cited his cancer as "rare and fast growing" he was transferred to Denver. He was put under the care of oncologist Dr. John Cullen of Presbyterian St. Luke's Hospital. Brad's family was driving to Denver at least once a week from their home in Rushville. In May of his junior year, just five months after his original diagnosis of cancer, doctors discovered a second cancer invading his body. This time it was germ cell cancer. "The doctors had never seen a patient with two kinds of cancer at the same time," Diane said. "It's

*not a comfort to the parents when the doctors are baffled."
The treatment for germ cell cancer was almost worst than
the disease. Brad went through four chemo sessions. Each
session included four, eight-hour days with drugs running
through his veins. He'd never been sicker in his life.*

"Effects of Treatment"

*Brad's cancer has now gone into remission, however
the damage of the aggressive treatments still pervade to
protect his immune system during the chemo sessions,
Brad was given high doses of steroids, the steroids caused
his bones and joints to deteriorate. "That was totally
unexpected," Diane said. "The doctors never told us that
might happen," Since the cancer diagnosis, Brad has gone
through ten surgeries, including two hip replacements.
With the help of physical therapy three times a week,
Brad is able to walk without a cane when he's not overly
tired. However, his knees are beginning to hurt, so knee
replacement surgery may be the next on the list. "Hip
replacements only last ten to fifteen year," Diane said.
"This will continue to effect Brad for the rest of his life."
Brad's not worried about the future, and he is not scared
of doctors. By now hospitals, needles and anesthesia are a
regular part of his life.*

"Support"

*Before cancer, Brad was your average high school student.
He loved attending athletic games and had a job at Ryan's
Market, the local grocery store. He also delivered the
Omaha World Herald daily. When the treatments and
sickness set in, Brad had to quit his job at the grocery*

store, but continued his paper route. At the beginning of his chemo sessions, Brad spent three weeks in Denver with his parents, and little sister, Kristin. To save his paper route, Brad's 28 classmates banded together and took turns delivering the paper. To save his grades, several teachers made personal trips to Brad's house to help him with missed school work. Thanks to these extra efforts, Brad was able to graduate with his class on May 13. The experience of cancer has also brought the Moore family closer together. "We've learned to appreciate every day," Diane said.

"Friends Along the Way"

Hot and fast cars are a must for teenage boys. Brad is no different. A fiery red 1967 Mustang sits in the Moore's driveway. The car belongs to Brad and comes with a story. Shortly after his second diagnosis with cancer, the family was driving through Chadron on their way home from Denver. The car, decorated with a "For Sale" sign, caught their attention and they pulled over for a closer look. They spoke with the owner, Scott Pearson, and told him they were making a lot of trips between Denver and Rushville. When Pearson learned that Brad had cancer, he surprised the Moore's with news of his own. His son, Jeffrey, was diagnosed with cancer at 5 days-old. Both Jeffrey and Brad were treated by Dr. Cullen at the same hospital. Jeffrey is now three and cured from the disease. Brad ended up buying the car from Pearson. "Now they are great friends of the family," Diane said. Brad also had a brush with fame. As a lifelong fan of the Cornhuskers football team, he was thrilled when he learned that receiver's coach Ron Brown was giving a speech at Chadron State College. Unfortunately, Brad was scheduled for a chemo treatment in Denver on that date. Another friend of the family knew how much Brad wanted to meet Ron Brown, so they arranged for Brown to come visit Brad at home. "I was really impressed with that," Lee said. "He's a good guy." Brad was delighted with the visit. Brown encouraged him to never give up and the two prayed together before he left.

"Future"

Brad won't be going to college in the fall. Right now his plans are to recover fully. However, his dreams do extend beyond the immediate future. Brad would like to be a radio D.J. He hopes to go to Chadron State College in the fall of 2002. Medical bills and traveling expenses have hindered the double income family. Though they have an insurance plan, it does not cover everything for Brads treatments. College funding could be a problem. A new scholarship made available by the American Caner Society could be of assistance. The scholarship is available for cancer victims who were diagnosed before the age of 21. A scholarship may give cancer victims the boost they need to reach higher education goals. Brad plans to fill out the scholarship application when it arrives in the mail.

"Coping"

Brad sees his youth as an advantage in the fight against cancer. "Older people can't bounce back as well," he says. Recently, Brad was the guest speaker at the Relay for Life. He proudly walked the survivor's lap with others who have fought the disease. "Lee and I are so proud of him. He's had such a great attitude throughout this," Diane said. It's no secret that cancer has altered Brad's life. Still, he tries not to think about it. He feels like a normal young man. He likes to hang out with friends, drive his car and watch sports. He's just fighting cancer in the meantime.

The next month, for my next doctor appointment, my cousin Jodi went with Mom and I. We checked into the hospital for X-rays and scans, and met with Dr. Cullen. My checkup went well and we headed back to Rushville, all in the same day.

During the fall, when the rest of my classmates were going off to college, I stayed home. It was just too soon for me, and I was still recuperating from surgery. I was not able to attend college because of the remaining chemotherapy treatments. So college was out of the question for me for the time being.

In late November, my dad and I were able to go to a Denver Broncos game. The Broncos played the Washington Redskins. We got the tickets from the Diane Price Fish Foundation. Our seats were way up high in the New Mile High Stadium, so we looked for an elevator or escalator to help me get up the steps. We could not find anything and were very frustrated. I tried walking up the massive amount of steps. The steps were steep, it was very cold and icy, and my hips were killing me. I had a hard time getting to my seat. It was a terribly cold day. It had been raining and sleeting. Both Dad and I dressed warm, but we did not have anything water resistant, so we both were pretty wet, cold, and miserable. We finally left in the third quarter. The Broncos were losing to the Redskins at that time; we both knew the Broncos were going to lose this game, and I probably should not have been there in the shape I was in. The next day, my mom and dad took me to see Dr. Cullen for my appointment. It went well and we drove home, thankful to be dry and warm.

Chapter 4

The College Years Begin

On January 4, 2002, it was my nineteenth birthday; my mom took me to Chadron State College to sign up for classes. It was a nice way to start the year and a great birthday gift. Later, my family and friends joined us for a pizza party.

Later that week it was off to Denver again to see Dr. Cullen and get a chemo treatment. I got along fine and did not get too sick.

On my next trip to Denver, in February, the doctors told me that they wanted to take the groshong out of my chest. It had been in there since January of 2000. That was good news to me! I remember feeling very excited that my health was improving. So that was a great day and it was nice to have it out of my chest.

On March 27, I was back in Denver again. This time, Dr. Kelly performed surgery on my left knee. It also had problems with avascular necrosis. She told me then that she wanted to wait until May to do the right knee. The day after surgery, Dr. Cullen told me that I was looking good. Physical therapy also came in and worked with me right away. I learned that each surgery was different to come back from. For me, knee surgery was harder than hip surgery because I could not bend my knee for a good three weeks, which was tough.

After I got home, Mom and Dad bought a new recliner for me so I could keep my legs propped up. Those surgeries were very hard on me and the new recliner was really nice. My parents also got me a wheelchair as well. As soon as I was able to, I was making regular trips to see Kim Marlett in Gordon for physical therapy.

On May 21, the whole family went to Denver for my pre-op appointment. That trip, we brought Tyler Fisher with us. Then we all went out to Dave & Buster's to eat. The next day, I had my right knee operated on. The surgery went as well as could be expected. Joe and Jerene came to visit again too. The surgeries were taking place like I had wanted. I knew I was going to start college in the fall so I wanted to get the knee surgeries done in the summer so I would have time to recuperate. Before we came home from Denver, all of us went to the Denver Zoo. Everyone took turns pushing me around the zoo in my wheelchair.

When I got home from Denver, I was back again, going to physical therapy in Gordon. Kim was glad to see me, and she and I both knew that I had a lot of work to do with the two knee surgeries.

At the end of June, Mom and I went to Chadron State College again to get a tour of the campus, meet some professors, and sign up for more classes. That week, we also attended the annual Relay for Life in Chadron. It must have been about 110 degrees that day! I managed to go around the track on my crutches just a couple of times.

During my doctor's appointment in Denver that July, Joe and Jerene took my family and me up to the mountains to Estes Park. It was really nice and a fun trip for all of us. It was especially fun for me to be able to do something enjoyable again while I was in Denver. There were so many times that Mom and I would go to my appointment and then just come straight home afterward. The next day, we all went to Six Flags Amusement Park. Kristin had a really good time, but I remember getting sick on some of the rides.

On August 4, our whole family left for Denver again. My checkup went well, which was really good news because college started that next week. All the doctors said that I was healthy enough to start college. I can remember them telling me how brave I was because of everything that I had overcome so far. Both Dr. Cullen and Dr. Kelly wished me well with college and admired my enthusiasm about starting.

In late August, I was able to finally start college at Chadron State, thirty miles from my hometown of Rushville. (Looking back on it now, having cancer probably influenced my decision to go to Chadron State, since it was so close to home.)

During my time at Chadron State, I tried not to let on to people I met that I was a current cancer patient. It worked pretty well, but it probably would have been easier if I did not have the hip and knee problems. I tried to walk right but had a definite limp because of the pain in my hips. I would only walk to class and back to my dorm room. Most of the time, I would drive my car to class just so that I would not have to walk much . . . and to make sure I would get there on time. If I did walk, I would make sure to take extra time so that I could sit down part way and rest as I was in terrible pain with my hips at that time.

I started college in the fall of 2002, a whole year later than my classmates from high school. I did not let that stop me. My parents moved me into the freshman dorms called Kent Hall. It was where the entire freshman class lived. The girls were on the top floor and boys on the bottom floor. It was quite an experience, and something that I might not have been ready for. You could stay up as late as you wanted, and you were not required to even go to class if you did not want to. I could have gotten caught up in all of the drinking and partying that a lot of freshmen did their first semester, but I did not. Maybe it was because of what I went through with cancer and everything else, or maybe I just had a good head on my shoulders. I think it was a combination of both.

Even before college, I was never a drinker. I chose not to drink, smoke, or use tobacco. I never did anything that broke the law. In my younger years, I was pretty sheltered, and college was a total culture shock to me. The party life was at my fingertips, and I chose not to get involved. I did meet a lot of cool friends. My next-door neighbor in Kent Hall was a kid from Hay Springs named Aaron Summers. He and I have a birthday only a day and a year apart. It turned out that he knew who I was because of my Mustang. He liked my car, and we started hanging out and became good friends. We are still really close friends today.

I enrolled in mostly general education classes that first year. I knew I wanted to be a radio DJ ever since sixth grade. But Chadron State did not have a radio program like other schools did. The closest they had was a Communications degree. It was a really good program at Chadron State, so that is what I majored in. I went for a minor in history.

During my first semester, I was in one of my Communications classes and I met a student named Andy Urlab. He was at least one year older than me. He asked me if I would be interested in pledging to a fraternity. He caught me by surprise; I was not sure about this. But I decided it might be a good way to meet some new people and make friends. So I told Aaron about it, and he seemed interested too. Aaron and I ended up pledging into Omega Phi Rho. It is a local, social fraternity that is based at Chadron State College.

Not all the stereotypes about fraternities are true. I told them that I did not want to drink, all of them respected my wishes, and I was never tempted to drink. Overall, I am really glad I joined the fraternity. I did meet some really good friends, and I still keep in touch with most of them. Just like high school, college was a great experience for me. I actually got better grades in college than I did in high school. This was probably because I tried harder in college.

On September 6, my family and I left to go to Lincoln for another Husker game and stayed at my Uncle Mike's apartment. On Saturday we all went to the game. It was Nebraska vs. Utah State. Nebraska won big, 44-13. It was also a great day to be at Memorial Stadium because the weather was so nice. We all had a wonderful time. On the way back, we visited my Aunt Trish and family in Grand Island. (When I got back to college, I took my Mustang back to Chadron to show off to my friends. They all really liked my car.)

My next doctor's appointment was set for December 8. Once again, our whole family made the trip. This time we took Uncle Mike. We were able to see an Aerosmith concert at the Pepsi Center. The next day we went to my appointment to see Dr. Cullen. When I got there, we found out that he had suddenly quit. This was very shocking to us! I had really liked him as a doctor. Lucky for me, I was mostly done with all of the hard stuff. I then was referred to Dr. Smith, and my family and I decided that I would just start going to see Dr. Packard in Scottsbluff full-time. Besides, he was the doctor I thought the world of. He was so caring and treated me so well.

Chapter 5

A Quiet Year

Two thousand and three proved to be the most uneventful year for me as far as my cancer and surgeries, which was really good. I can remember going to all of my scheduled doctor's appointment and having a good report the whole year.

On February 19, I went to state wrestling in Lincoln to help out with reporting matches for the KCSR sports team. That was really fun and made me even more aware of how I liked being in the radio business. Rushville won their third straight state championship in wrestling.

In early August, my friend Aaron invited me to go to the Black Hills to the Sturgis Bike Rally. I met Aaron at Hermosa, South Dakota, and then followed him to Sturgis, where he was staying. I even made arrangements to drive my dad's pickup so I could haul my bicycle in the back. I knew that would be the only way I could get around Sturgis, as my hips were bothering me so much. Aaron worked that summer at Crystal Cave as a tour guide. After I saw some wild sights at the famous bike rally, Aaron took me through a guided tour of Crystal Cave. The tours were about twenty to thirty minutes long. At this time, my hips were probably hurting me worse than they ever had been, but I always tried not to let my hip problem get in the way of having fun and doing things with friends.

When I went on the tour of the cave with Aaron, I tried to be Mr. Tough Guy and did not tell him how bad my hips really hurt me. It did not take long before both of my legs were just shaking. Aaron did not know what to do other than just feel bad. Mom and Dad were already in the area, as they were on their way back from the Black Hills. They had decided to surprise me and stop at Crystal Cave to see Aaron and me. When Aaron saw my parents, he was really worried about me and told them that I was still in the cave and he was unable to get me out. By that time, I was in excruciating pain and my legs were visibly shaking out of control with muscle spasms. I was in a mess! Aaron didn't know how he was going to get me on my feet again, plus he had his job to do, guiding others through the cave. When my parents arrived, he ended up bringing my dad into the cave, and then the two of them were able to help me get to my feet. With my muscle spasms completely out of control, Aaron and Dad tried to carry me. Somehow this hurt even worse! So I ended up walking as slowly as I could, holding tight to my dad's arms. I was in constant pain with each step. Once I got close to the exit, my mom, who was at the cave entrance wondering what was taking us so long to come out, started yelling my name. Maybe it was a mix of emotions and some of the worst pain ever, but I started to cry when I heard my mom. Back then, my legs not only hurt whenever I walked a short distance, but my muscles would just spasm out of control and that hurt maybe the most. This was a case of a friend not knowing how bad off I was as I really never told even my closest friends that I was a cancer patient and that I had gone through hip surgeries. I never wanted any attention drawn to me and wanted my friends to just think I was "normal." I learned from this experience, that it did not pay to keep the condition of how bad my hips were from a friend that was giving me a guided tour. I was in no condition to be in that cave in the first place. But I never wanted any attention drawn to me and wanted my friends to just think I was normal. My pride was just in the way. This was an experience that I will never forget; it also made it really clear that the temporary fix to my hips was wearing off quicker than the orthopedic surgeon ever expected it would.

I met with Dr. Packard just before I went back to college for my second year. He told me that I was doing really well, there was no sign of cancer at the moment, and I was in good health. I felt pretty good that year, expect for my hips, which were constantly bothering me. But with my determination and stubbornness, I never let my hip problems stand in the way of going to a Husker game. I ended up going to the Nebraska vs. Penn State football game that year. Nebraska won that game 18-10.

In the fall of 2003, I had an internship at KCSR radio station in Chadron for college credit. This was perfect for me because radio broadcasting was what I really wanted to get into. That fall, I helped out with high school football by keeping stats and doing some sports reporting. I also helped out with taking pictures during basketball season. I really enjoyed that experience.

Chapter 6

My Third Cancer Diagnosis

On January 4th, once Once again y family and I went to Rapid City to celebrate my twenty-first birthday. Later that month, my whole family went to Lincoln to see my Uncle Mike graduate from the Nebraska State Trooper School.

In March, during spring break 2004, I went to Utah with friends from college, my fraternity brothers from Omega Phi Rho. Clay Milburn, who was a member of the fraternity, worked at a ski resort in Utah and invited all of us to go out there to stay for a few days. I can remember not being able to ski because of my hips and knee problems, but I was still able to enjoy myself by watching my friends. We all got pretty sunburned!

In early June, I had an appointment with Dr. Packard in Scottsbluff. Tests showed that my thymus was enlarged. Dr. Packard said he would do more tests during my next appointment and not to worry about it. That was almost impossible for my mom! At my next appointment in August, Dr. Packard ordered a PET scan. This type of scan was more detailed than the CAT scan that I usually had. The results showed a problem with my thyroid. Further testing was confirmed I had thyroid cancer. Here I was, three years later, and diagnosed with yet another type of cancer, still unrelated to the other two. This was my third malignancy! Dr. Packard said I would need a biopsy done on my neck. After the biopsy, Dr. Packard told me officially that it was thyroid cancer (hurthle cell tumor).

After all that news, it was time for college to start back up again. This was Kristin's first year of college, while I was entering my third year. The doctors said I would only need surgery to take care of the thyroid cancer; no chemo was needed. This made me very happy. I had already missed a lot of high school. I did not want to miss college too.

On August 27, I had the surgery done in Scottsbluff. Dr. Forney removed the left side of my thyroid. He said the surgery went well. He also told us the tumor was encapsulated and that he was 95-8 percent sure it was benign. Later that week, Dr. Packard called and told my family and me that he had my surgery results. He had them sent to a pathologist in New York because the results looked suspicious.

In early September, I went back to Scottsbluff for another surgery on my thyroid. The first time Dr. Forney did surgery, they decided to only take half of my thyroid, and then they would do more testing. Well, after the first surgery, I woke up and could not talk. It was really bad, because my dream job was to be a sports announcer. We went to some specialists, and they told me that there was damage done to my vocal chords during surgery and I might have trouble talking. At that time, I could only whisper. But as time went on, I got my voice back. Then the test results confirmed it was malignant.

On September 11, my dad and I had tickets to the Nebraska football game. It was the first year for new head coach Bill Callahan. Nebraska got upset by Southern Mississippi by a score of 21-17. In my opinion, if Nebraska would have stuck to the running game as a game plan, the Huskers may not have lost to the Golden Eagles of Southern Mississippi. I was not even able to shout and cheer for my beloved Huskers because of the surgery on my thyroid.

After I got back from Lincoln, my mom and I went to an ear, nose, and throat specialist. I was told I had permanent damage to the left side of my vocal chords. That doctor said there was 75 percent damage to my vocal chords! I was devastated and so was my mom! Dr. Forney called off the surgery for the right side and said we could get a second opinion. He said he would not put his own son through a second surgery and that I should just leave my thyroid alone. After my appointment with the ear, nose, and throat specialist, Dr. Forney called my mom to apologize and said he couldn't believe it was permanent damage as he thought everything went well. He did not think he nicked my vocal chords during surgery.

On October 14, I was all set to have the other side of my thyroid removed, but the surgery was later called off. Finally, Dr. Packard called and said he wanted to wait until my November appointment to do some more testing and then decide if surgery would be done in December.

Then on December 21, Dr. Packard decided it would be in my best interest if they did another surgery and removed the other side of my thyroid. I can remember this surgery being one of the only surgeries that I was ever afraid of having because of the fear that my voice would possibly be lost forever.

I was later told that Dr. Forney even came out, talked to me and my mom, and guaranteed me that I would not lose my voice. He was right. I woke up from the surgery, Mom asked me to talk, and I did. So, since the doctors took my thyroid out, this meant I would have to take a thyroid replacement pills once a day for the rest of my life. I thought that would be a very small price to pay and was happy that was all I had to do.

Chapter 7

A Painful Year

It was now 2005 and I celebrated my twenty-second birthday with my family and some friends, on January fourth. Soon after, it was time for college classes to start up again. On January 10, I had doctor appointments with both Dr. Forney and Dr. Packard. I was given a good report from both doctors and was told my scar was healing well. This was just one more to add to my already scarred up body.

The months went by fast when I was in college. I kept busy with classes and being with friends. Before I knew it, it was April and the Huskers had a spring game. My dad and I attended. This was the first time that I had ever been to a spring football game in Lincoln. I really had a hard time walking to our seats in the stadium. I was in so much pain; I had to take breaks and nearly had to be carried. I really should not have been at that game in the shape I was in, but I was determined to go and would endure the pain! In order for me to take a step, I would often have to grab my pant leg for assistance. This was what it had come to. I was in serious need of a total hip replacement.

In early May, just after classes let out for the summer at Chadron State College, my mom and I went to see Dr. Packard for a checkup. He told me that he was going to adjust my dosage of thyroid medicine and it would be changed soon. I told him that I was signed up for a college class that required a field trip to the Black Hills. He said I could go but I would need to come back afterward to see him for another appointment to get the dosage exactly right.

During the first week in June, I enrolled in a class called "Becoming the Black Hills," which required a class field trip to the Black Hills in South Dakota and an overnight stay in Deadwood. The class went toward my History minor. It was about two weeks long, then a trip to the Black Hills, to complete the rest of the requirements. This should not have really mattered that I went on this trip; it would have been fine and just a normal trip for the average person. No big deal, right? Not for me. I ended up having a lot of problems. My thyroid was acting up and doctors were in the process of deciding my medication dosage. So, during the trip, I started not feeling well. The first night I was there, I went to walk around in the casino across the street, and some college friends were there. (My friends wanted to take me to a bachelor party in Rapid City, which was about forty-five minutes away from Deadwood. So, I went with them.) We got back pretty late that night, and the next day was a full day of class work, like touring museums and going to a historic graveyard called Mount Moriah. It is in Deadwood and is where some of the famous Wild West heroes, like Wild Bill, are all buried. Everything that was planned was just too much for me. I made it to Mount Moriah but could barely walk. I told my teacher that I needed to sit down and rest. She agreed. She also said I did not look well and was very pale. I felt every bit the way I looked. It must have been a combination of things that made me feel that way. It was probably from not getting a good night's sleep before, all the walking, and my thyroid not working properly.

I can remember that day as being so miserable for me. With my thyroid acting up, it made me feel really drained, with no energy. It was also hot out, and my hips were really hurting. It was a very bad combination of everything. My system just shut down. I had someone help me sit down after we went to Mount Moriah and getting back on the bus. At the next stop, our class was going to tour the historic Adams House Museum. I was too sore to even go into the museum. I was able to make it to a park bench in front of the museum, and I watched my legs as they just shook from muscle spasms. It was very painful. I was used to this type of pain, but that day it was the worst I can remember. I was also used to my hips limiting me from doing so much during that time. Most of the time, I knew my limits, but that day I ended up way over-doing it.

It was a very crazy coincidence that the friends I saw in the casino were my friends from Omega Phi Rho. I did not know they were there. They were in Deadwood celebrating my friend Heath's wedding, so they took him there to have a bachelor party. Looking back on that now, I should have never gone with those guys to Rapid City. But just like so many times before, I did not use good judgment and thought I would be able to deal with it. That next day was still probably one of the most painful days of my life.

Later that month, Mom and I went to see Dr. Packard to get my dosage corrected for my thyroid medicine. I told him about my trip to the Black Hills and the hard time I had with my thyroid and hips acting up on me. He really felt bad for me and told me that he would adjust my dosage and believed that would help me.

Summer went by fast, and soon college classes were starting at Chadron State. I was beginning my junior year in college. During the first week of classes, while attending a history class, I met Josh McLain, who later became my best friend. After only a few days of knowing each other, Josh invited me to his house. When I walked in, I was greeted by his mom. She had made cookies for us. After I got to know Josh, I found out that he was the oldest of six kids whose names all began with the letter J. I also found out later that Josh's brother was the starting quarterback for the Chadron State Eagles and that he had two more brothers in high school who were also quarterbacks. He also had two sisters who were great athletes. I was truly lucky to meet such a great family. I have gotten to know the whole McLain family, and every one of them is very nice. Josh and his family are truly blessings in my life. I am glad to call them my special friends.

In early September, I was complaining to my mom that my hips were still hurting. Sometimes, it was so bad I just didn't want to do anything or try to walk anywhere. The pain was severe. She made an appointment to see the orthopedic surgeon in Scottsbluff for an opinion on total hip replacement. He told me the same thing I had been told before: that I was too young" for total hip replacement. So, I had to live with the pain. I would sometimes take pain pills to just get through the day. The other way I dealt with it was to do as little as possible. I tried to limit my walking as much as I could. I was experiencing muscle spasms in my legs on a daily basis.

On October 1, my family got tickets to a Husker game in Lincoln. Nebraska played Iowa State. The Huskers won that game 27-20, in overtime. It was the first overtime game I had ever been at and it was very exciting. I was thrilled to be there! At this game, I felt pretty good: my thyroid medication was now adjusted, my hips were still a problem, but I don't remember over-doing it that day.

In November, it was time for the annual Relay for Life. I formed a team again. This year, some fraternity guys came and walked with my family and me. I went around to local business and got donations. We had a raffle to raise money for cancer research. My fraternity brothers banded together to raise money too and formed a team in my honor. They walked around the track all night long. This was my fourth year walking as a survivor.

Fraternity Brother's helping out at the "Relay for Life"

Here is a story that was printed in the *Chadron Record* November, 2005:

Fraternity Supports Cancer Survivor at Relay for Life

Brad Moore of Chadron went to the hospital in January of 2000 with a sore a neck, just three days before his 17th birthday. Several days later, Brad, his family and a group of college friends began an experience that would change lives. Brad Was diagnosed with lymphoma, the first of three cancers he has overcome in the past five years. This past week at the Relay for Life, over 200 people supported cancer research by continually walking at the 12-hour event. They also honored the memories of those claimed by cancer and celebrated with the survivors, including Brad. "Brad has a very positive outlook on life," said his mother, Diane. "He would like to put his cancer experience in his past and look to his future in sports announcing." This will be the fourth year that Brad has participated in Chadron's Relay for Life. Also, inspired by Brad's cancer were members from his local "Omega Phi Ro" fraternity, who attended the event for the second year. The fraternity members not only walked, they also raffled items to raise funds for cancer research. The items included a satellite radio, a $50.00 gift certificate and scented candles. Omega Phi Ro members also went to area businesses to raise money for cancer awareness. They've raised $140.00 by waiting tables and washing dishes at a fund raiser at "Pizza Ranch." "I think it's wonderful." Diane said about the group's efforts. "I think it's neat that a group of guys would support Brad." Those who know Brad would not know about his experiences with cancer: including his fellow fraternity members. "We're proud *to walk,. "said Steve Hagen, the President of Omega Phi Ro Chadron fraternity. "You can't find a better guy than Brad." Hagen said that he had been around Brad for several years and the fraternity is a tight knit group. But, Brad fought his battle with cancer without alerting many to his condition. A great amount of time passed before other fraternity members knew about Brad's cancer. "I first found out on the way home from State Wrestling," Hagen said. He knew Brad for several months before that point. When diagnosed with Lymphoma in 2000, Brad regularly traveled to Presbyterian St. Luke's Hospital in Denver for his chemotherapy treatments. He was sick from the chemotherapy and coping with the new diagnosis when four months later, he was diagnosed with a second cancer that was unrelated to his first diagnosis. The family spent many days on the road between Rushville and Denver in order for Brad to receive his chemo treatments.*

"His oncologist in Denver said, this was a very rare care and put his first cancer treatment 'on hold'" while he treated Brad aggressively with chemo for his second diagnosis," said Diane. Brad was given steroids to give him strength to endure the drugs to fight the cancer. The steroids caused 'avascular necrosis' in both of Brad's hips and also both knees. He missed many days of school during this time. Shortly after starting his senior year of high school in Rushville, Brad found out about his hip problems. He had his first hip surgery in September of his senior year and spent many days on crutches, but was able to walk across the stage to receive his diploma along with his class of 2001. Two days after his graduation, he was back in Denver for his second hip surgery. He spent most of the next year recuperating from two hip and two knee surgeries. "He was not able to go to college when

his classmates did, but with his determination, positive attitude and many hours of physical therapy, Brad managed to start college at Chadron State in the fall of 2002," said Diane. Brad is not able to do the things he used to, like being involved in sports, and is limited on how long he can be on his feet. But he loves to watch events Diane said, and, is taking communication classes at CSC with the goal of becoming a sports announcer/radio DJ. He continued to do well in college and felt well before September of 2004. Brad was then diagnosed with his third malignancy; thyroid cancer. He opted to have surgery done during Christmas break of 2004, so that he would not have to miss any college classes. He is now in remission and continues to see his oncologist for checkups. Brad is optimistic about his recovery and is thankful for all of the support he has received. "It's an experience I wouldn't wish on anyone," Brad said. "But we've had a lot of support from family and friends." Brad said that his community and church have been especially helpful in his treatments and recuperation. "You can learn to deal with cancer," Brad said. "Keep a positive attitude and never give up!"

Chapter 8

College Graduation

I celebrated my twenty-third birthday on January 4, 2006, by being with my family and friends. College classes were just around the corner. I was extra excited because this was my last year of college.

After the semester was over, I enrolled in more summer classes. I had always lived in the dorms on campus, even in the summer months. I heard about an apartment off-campus that came open. I called about it and was able to move in on the first of June. This apartment was good for me because it was all on one level. I had no steps to deal with and had off-street parking for my car. I was glad to have my own place!

On June 10, I went to my grandparents fiftieth anniversary. Our whole family was there. It was the first time in a long time that I had a chance to see all my aunts, uncles, and cousins. During this fun event, I was able to make it through with no pain.

Later that month, the youth group at church had a celebration for our youth leader Darrell Johnson, to honor him. He was an amazing man, and I am glad I got to know him. He was in poor health at the time, and we all wanted to show our appreciation to him for being such a fun, caring youth leader.

My summer college classes were soon going to start, so Mom went with me to an appointment with Dr. Packard.

I had another PET scan to check my thyroid to make sure everything was normal, and I got a good report.

On August 24, I sold my big-screen TV that I received through the Make-A-Wish-Foundation to a family in Gordon. I thought that was the best thing I could do. Because of the technology of big screen TVs, it was in my best interest to get a different one. I used the money from the old one to buy a brand-new big screen TV. I still have the surround-sound system, carts, and speakers, and will always be thankful for the gift I received from them.

On September 9, Josh invited me to go with him and his family to Montana. We went to watch Chadron State play against Montana State University. This matched CSC against a division higher than Chadron. Montana State, just the week before, had upset a division higher than them, the Colorado Buffalos. So the McLain family and I traveled to Bozeman, Montana, to watch the underdog Eagles play. Chadron State ended up winning the game 31-24 over the heavily favored Bobcats, thanks to two-time Harlen Hill winner and former Chadron State great Danny Woodhead, who was the Eagles' running back at the time.

The McLain family really took me under their wing, and I got to travel with them to almost all the away football games. I even made trips with Josh and his family to North Dakota, where they are originally from. They are like a second family to me.

In September, my dad got a new job with Burlington Northern Santa Fe Railroad. Even though he had just started a new job, he took me to a Husker game in Lincoln on September 30. For the second straight year, the game went into overtime as the Cornhuskers defeated the Kansas Jayhawks 39-32.

On December 2, I left with the McLain family to see a Chadron State playoff game in Maryville, Missouri, the home of Northwest Missouri State. My friends Kory and JoAnna also went with us. We then left after that game to go to the Big 12 Championship Husker game in Kansas City, Missouri, at Arrowhead Stadium. It was very cold at both games and my hips were hurting pretty bad, but I did not let that stop me from having a good time. I kept myself doped up on pain pills just so I could just go to those games. Unfortunately, both Chadron State and Nebraska lost.

After I got back from the football games, Mom and I went to Denver to see Dr. Kelly. I told her how bad my hips hurt all the time and how I would have trouble walking to my college classes. I could not get very far without them hurting me and going into muscle spasms. She X-rayed both my hips, saw the damage, and decided after I graduated from college, she would do the total hip replacement. Finally, I had a doctor who said she would do the surgery that I had wanted for so long! I was very excited. She told me that she would do the left hip first, let me recuperate from that, and then do the right hip. Looking back on it now, I went six years with bad hips. All that time, the doctors kept telling me that I was too young for total hip replacement. The worst of my hip pain did not start until 2003 or 2004. The temporary fix, which Dr. Kelly had done in Denver in September of 2000 on my left hip and in May 2001 on my right hip, worked for a while. But it got to be so bad that I was unable to walk a city block without being in pain. That's like going to Wal-Mart and not being able to make it to the electronics section. Something needed to be done, and be done soon, or I was going to have to be in a wheelchair. In fact, most of the time, back then, I even wanted to be in a wheelchair, because of the intense pain in my hips.

Finally, December 15 came: this was a big day for me! I graduated from Chadron State College. My family hosted a graduation party at my apartment. We had a really good turnout. A couple of days later my mom hosted another graduation party for me at my home in Rushville. We had another great turnout.

My Mom and I on Graudation Day

After I graduated, I did not waste any time. Mom and I went to my consultation appointment in Denver to see Dr. Kelly and find out how soon I could have the surgery done. She told me the left hip would be scheduled for January 10. She wanted me to recover from the left hip surgery and come back in March for the right hip. On the way back from Denver, we stopped in Scottsbluff to see Dr. Packard. I told him about the surgery and he agreed that I had suffered long enough.

He thought it was great that I finally got to have the surgery done.

Chapter 9

Finally—Total Hip Replacement!"

For my twenty-fourth birthday, in 2007, my mom and dad took me out for supper. I celebrated with my friend Aaron too; his birthday was the day before. We all had a good time.

One January 9, Mom and I left for Denver. My surgery was set for the next day. Joe and Jerene, our special angels, met with us and took us out to eat.

Finally, it was the day for my total hip replacement. I can remember wanting this surgery for such a long time. It might sound weird, but I was excited to get new hips. On January 10, I had a total hip replacement done on my left hip. Dr. Kelly said she had to chisel out the old piece and replace it with the whole ball and socket. Joe and Jerene stayed with my mom during the surgery. I even asked Dr. Kelly if I could have the piece that she chiseled out of my hip bone. I still have it today as a souvenir! She said I was considered to be the very youngest in history (at least there in Denver, at Presbyterian St. Luke's Hospital) to have a total hip replacement.

The next day, Dr. Kelly came in to check on me. She said I looked pretty good. Physical therapy came in and tried to get me to walk, but I just couldn't do it. I was too dizzy. After the physical therapist left, Joe and Jerene came to visit me. They stayed and visited for a quite a while.

On January 12, I was able to get up and walk just to the door of my room. I was getting better every day and I was determined to do whatever physical therapy told me to do. I wanted to walk again, with no pain! Dr. Kelly ordered a CAT scan to check for blood clots in my lungs. The scan came back clean. The next day, Dr. Kelly ordered an ultrasound on my legs and the report was good as well. My dad came to Denver to help drive us home. I got dismissed around noon and the roads were snowy and icy all the way home. We made it back to Chadron okay, but Mom stayed at my apartment for a couple of days to help me out. Mom also arranged for a home health nurse and a physical therapist to come to my apartment to work with me too. The next day, Grandma and Grandpa Cerny came to see me. By January 22, I was able to walk with crutches and get around better by myself.

Then on February 15, I went with Josh to North Dakota for a Fighting Sioux hockey game. Mom was thinking that it was too soon to go on a trip, but we both had fun. We stayed in Martin, South Dakota with Josh's grandparents on the way there. When we got to North Dakota, we stayed with Josh's other grandparents. I had a really good time on this trip, even though Mom was right: it was a little too soon for me to have been doing so much.

At the end of February, I got to meet with Ron Brown and Stan Parker again. They were at a church in Chadron to talk about putting up a tower to promote their Christian radio station. It was great to see them again and listen to their encouragement.

Later that month, I had an appointment in Scottsbluff to see Dr. Packard. I had another good checkup, and then left for Denver for a checkup with Dr. Kelly. Mom and I met up with Joe and Jerene for supper. My checkup with Dr. Kelly went well. She said I was doing great and gave me the A-okay to get my right hip done as soon as I wanted to! Mom and I drove home feeling pretty good about things. I was excited.

On March 13, Mom and I left for Denver for my right hip surgery. We met up with Joe and Jerene again for supper. Surgery on my right hip went well, just as expected. Dr. Kelly had to chisel out the old piece on this hip too. I was able to save it for a souvenir also. The next day, the physical therapist came, but I was too weak to get out of bed. Every day after that, I was determined to work as much as I could on walking and getting around. Dr. Kelly said I was doing great, and the physical therapist was amazed at my determination. On March 18, I got dismissed from the hospital. I even got interviewed by the local TV station about being the youngest patient to have both hips replaced.

Mom and I made it back to Chadron that next day. She took the whole week off from work to take care of me at my apartment. Soon the home health nurse and the physical therapist all came to my apartment to work with me again. I got better each day, and the physical therapist was amazed at how well I had improved. By March 23, I joked around with her and said, "I'm used to this by now."

By that time, I was a pro at surgery. I was not scared at all; in fact, I knew all the doctors and nurses, and more important, the anesthesiologist! You see, this is the guy you want to get in good with, because he gives you these awesome drugs that make you all loopy before surgery. This affects people differently, but in my case, I would have the best dreams, and they would be so realistic. For example, I woke up once after surgery and of course the first person I saw was my mom. She's the best! She later told me that I was telling her some pretty weird things. I really remember this one time in Denver when I woke up from surgery and my pastor, Harlen Wheeler, and his son, Matt, drove to Denver to surprise me after surgery. I woke up telling them all about the Civil War and that I had been in a battle, and our side won the war. They looked at me and started laughing. I also remember dreaming that I was a Nebraska football player and I had caught a pass from Eric Crouch that won the game!

By the end of March, I was almost back to normal. My hips were healing really well, and I was able to get around better. On April 15, I went back home to Rushville for Mom's birthday. Later in May, Mom and I left for Denver to see Dr. Kelly for a checkup of both my hips. She was shocked by how well and fast I had recovered. She told me that I was all better but I would never be able to run or jump or do anything that could hurt my hips. She told me if I was very careful, my hips could possibly last me for fifteen to twenty years.

In late July, I had an appointment with Dr. Packard for a checkup. He was also shocked by how fast I had recovered from both those major surgeries and was pleased at how well I was doing.

On September 1, our whole family went to the Husker game in Lincoln. This was a graduation gift to me from Chuck and Cindy Squire. Chuck was the superintendent of Rushville High while I was in high school. He also was on the chain gang during Nebraska football games for years and had great season tickets. That day, the Huskers played the University of Nevada and won big, 52-10.

Later in September, I went to El Paso, Texas, with Mike Bourne, a good friend from high school. We met up to go to Jon Henry's wedding; it was a great trip. I met Mike in Ogallala, Nebraska, and then Mike and I and his girlfriend Christian drove for fifteen hours straight, only stopping for gas. Jon was so happy that we made the trip to see him get married. It was a fun trip for me, and for the first time in a long time, my hips did not hurt me!

On November 22, my friend Josh and I left to go to Boulder, Colorado, for a Nebraska football game. I won two tickets to this game by entering a drawing on the Chadron State campus. The tickets included a hotel stay. We ended up staying at a really fancy hotel, and even the Colorado Buffalo's football team stayed there. I remember Josh said hi to the head coach, Dan Hawkins. Nebraska really should have won that game, but lost 65-51. We were very disappointed in the loss, but Josh and I had a great time. Coach Bill Callahan was fired shortly after that game.

As Josh and I drove back from Colorado, talking about the Husker loss, we both knew that Chadron State had a playoff game coming up really soon. On November 24, I met up with Josh and his family to watch Chadron State play Abilene Christian Wildcats in the Division II Football playoffs. This game would prove to be very entertaining and high-scoring. Entering the fourth quarter, the score was 49-20, with Abilene Christian holding a commanding lead. It looked like CSC was beat and beat badly. The fourth quarter came and the Eagles scored six times to tie the score at 56 and force overtime. The two teams traded scores in the overtime period. Then, on the Wildcats' last possession, the Eagles were able to hold them to a field goal. So, that meant Chadron State would need to score a touchdown to win the game. Quarterback Joe McLain scored the winning touchdown and the Eagles won 76-73. It was probably the best football game that I had ever seen.

Chapter 10

My Trip of a Lifetime

On January 1, 2008, Mom and Dad brought dinner up to my apartment, and then we left for Scottsbluff to see Uncle Mike and Aunt Courtney and brand-new baby Leah. For my birthday on the fourth, the whole family went to Rapid City. We came back and had cake and ice cream with friends and then watched the bowl game that night. Later that week, Mom and I went back to Scottsbluff to see Dr. Packard for a checkup. Once again, I had a good report.

In February, I was invited to the Chadron State football banquet as a special guest. Head Coach Bill O'Boyle heard about my cancer experience and wanted to honor me. He said I was an inspiration to others. The coach read a brief story about me being a cancer survivor and a huge football fan, especially of the CSC Eagles. I then got to stand up with the entire Chadron State senior class. Most of them gave me a hug and words of encouragement, and some people were even crying. It was a pretty emotional day for me, and quite an honor to be asked to be there! After that, I was presented with the helmet that my parents had bought for me at Darrell Johnson's benefit. It had been signed by Danny Woodhead. I was also presented with a CSC football jersey.

Me with Chadron State Head Football Coach Bill O'Boyle taken in 2008

On February 18, I went back to Rushville to spend the day with Mom since she had the day off. I went out on the back deck and slipped on some ice. I fell down the stairs—and broke my ankle! I was in so much pain. I was no stranger to pain with all the surgeries I had to have, but breaking my ankle was probably the worst pain ever. I can remember after I fell down the stairs, I had to get up and go back up the stairs into the house where my mom was. She had no idea I had fallen. I was a mess. When I got into the house, I think I just passed out from the pain. Mom then drove me to Chadron, where I was told my ankle was broke. I was just sick hearing that news. I was first, put in a walking cast. I later saw Dr. McLain, and he put a regular cast on me. I was told I had to wear it for six weeks and stay off my foot. So there I was . . . on crutches again! I could not even drive my car. It was a very depressing time for me. All of my other surgeries were planned out and I knew they were coming; this time, it was not expected and was even harder to deal with. Now for some reason, my left side of my body has always been the first to give me trouble. It was my left arm that got burned by a hot Tootsie Roll. It was on the left side of my body that the cancer in my neck started. It was my left hip that collapsed first. It was my left testicle that had to be removed. It was my left side of my thyroid that was cancerous. Pretty weird, huh? The scar on my stomach even curves to the left, and I am not even left handed. Maybe now, the curse is gone from my left side since I broke my right ankle. I hope so!

For the next week or so, Mom stayed home with me to help me out. The first day she went back to work, she got a call that Dad was in an accident and nearly cut his finger off. So she took me with her, and we ended up taking Dad to Scottsbluff for surgery. It was a bad week for all of us! I have probably had more surgeries then most people will have in their lifetime, but I'd never had a broken bone until my ankle.

After I got my cast off, I got a job working at Your Selling Team. I could not find a job doing what I wanted to do, radio broadcasting, so I took a job working at a call center in Chadron. My job was to call businesses in California to try to get an appointment with the IT director so the sales representative from the company could meet with them and try to sell computer products. A few of my friends worked there before me, and they all said it was a pretty good job. I was hired in April and I soon got the hang of the job and liked it. I was making about eighty calls a day. One day, my friend and I had a contest on who could make the most calls in one day, and I made 130 calls, but he made close to 150.

In May, Kristin graduated from Chadron State College with a degree in Education. My family hosted a graduation party for her at my apartment. She had a good turnout.

Kristin and I at Kristin's Graduation Party

In July, I had my usual checkup with Dr. Packard. I had a CAT scan and a PET scan. They both came back clean as a whistle.

I bought some used equipment from a high school friend in August and started a DJ business. I called it "Moore Music." I soon was getting bookings for weddings. Since then, I've had the opportunity to buy even more equipment and my side business has grown.

On September 6, Josh and I left after the Chadron State football game and took a trip to Minneapolis, Minnesota. We stayed with his aunt and uncle who lived there. The next day, we traveled to Green Bay, Wisconsin, to see the first Monday night football game of the season. This game matched the Packers against the Vikings, who had a heated rivalry. The game was supposed to feature the retirement of longtime Packers quarterback, Brett Favre. But just before the start of the 2008 season, Favre got picked up by the New York Jets. Josh and I really enjoyed that game. The Packers won 24-19.

During the same trip, we checked to see if there was a baseball game playing while we were there. The Minnesota Twins had a home game the next day, so we went. The Twins also won their game. It was a great trip and we had a lot of fun!

On October 3, Mom, Kristin, and I went to Lincoln to a Husker football game. We met up with my two aunts and cousins, and stayed with cousin Justina in Lincoln. Nebraska played Missouri that game; Nebraska lost this game 52-17. This was the first time since 1978 Missouri beat Nebraska in Lincoln. We had a good trip but it was an emotional letdown for me.

Kristin and I at a Nebraska Football Game

In November, Josh and I went back to Minneapolis. This time we met up with Josh's younger brother, Jake, and some of his friends from North Dakota. We went to another football game. This time the Vikings were playing at home against the Packers. Josh and I got our tickets really early and paid a little more. We got tickets that put us in the second row. Since we were so close, Mom made us a sign that said, "Nebraskans for Minnesota." We were hoping that might get us on TV. We did make it on the Metro Dome TV during some crowd shots, but not on national TV like we had hoped. It was a really exciting game; the Vikings won 28-27. Josh, his brothers, and I went to his uncle's house after the game for dinner. Then we drove fifteen hours straight through, all the way home to Chadron. We only stopped for gas and food. It was a long trip, but again, Josh and I had a great time!

Both Josh and I were going to a lot of sports games together, but we really had our sights on going to a Nebraska Bowl Game. We both knew that it would be a big trip. I was watching the Nebraska-Colorado game the day after Thanksgiving, and when Nebraska kicked that 57-yard field goal to beat Colorado 40-31. I knew then, that I wanted to go to the Bowl Game. We did not even know who they were going to play or where the game was going to be, but Josh and I both knew we wanted to go. My parents and Josh's parents were both against us going, as they all thought we had been to enough games for the year—plus, they didn't think we would be able to afford it. Both Josh and I would rather starve for a month and do without groceries, just to save money so we could go. We didn't care if we paid our rent for the month nor had gas in our cars; we just wanted to go to that game!

When we both found out that Nebraska was playing in Florida, in the Gator Bowl, we knew that we just *had* to go. It was a great opportunity to do this while we were young and both single. We talked his dad into helping us find a package deal to go to Florida, which included getting a plane, hotel, game tickets, and a car to rent, all for about $700. I had some money saved up for a long time, so I used that. That trip, to this day, is the greatest trip I have ever taken! We left December 28 and got back on January 3, the day before my twenty-sixth birthday. We also spent New Year's Eve with about one hundred thousand strangers who were mostly Clemson Fans and some Husker Fans too. Josh planned the whole trip. He said we could go see the Atlantic Ocean, so we traveled to a nice resort in South Carolina, called Hilton Head Island. That was the first time I had ever seen any ocean. The next day was the football game. We went to our seats, looked around, and saw all of the orange and red.

There was not much scoring in the first half of the game—though there was plenty of excitement in the second-half! Nebraska and Clemson changed scores a couple of times. The game came down to the end. Nebraska was winning, but Clemson had the football at Nebraska's 30-yard line, and if they would score a touchdown, they would win. It came down to 4th down. The pass sailed incomplete. Nebraska won the game 26-21! I don't think I have ever been more excited than at that time. It was a moment I will never forget!

Me and Josh McLain at the Gator Bowl

The next day, Josh and I drove to Daytona Beach. This was a more public beach than the one in Hilton Head Island. Daytona was really cool. There were people everywhere. We put close to five hundred miles on the rental car. It was really worth all of the money I spent on that trip.

Josh McLain and I at the Alantic Ocean

Chapter 11

American Broadcasting School

I celebrated the new year 2009 with my friend Josh. When I got back from Florida, my family had planned a surprise birthday party for me. All of Josh's brothers came to my party, along with a few of my other friends. I felt really good and was so happy I was able to go on that trip. I was also very thankful I had such a great family and friends.

On February 6, I got laid off from my job at Your Selling Team. I was very disappointed at first because, I showed up for work every day and did my best. I did not get a lot of sales, but that was because when I called, I got the answering machine most of the time. I worked through Christmas and then the company made cutbacks. I was still one of the newer employees and so I got laid off. I worked there from April 2008 to February 2009, almost a year.

Losing my job really made me want to search for radio-broadcasting jobs. I went to the radio station in Chadron. They had a full staff and wanted someone with radio experience. I have a college degree from Chadron State College in Communication Arts, but there was no hands-on training for a day-to-day radio disc jockey. So I got on the internet and found an on-line broadcasting school called American Broadcasting School based out of Oklahoma City, Oklahoma.

I called and asked about taking classes. I was excited to start my on-line classes later that fall.

During my down time, I took advantage of having time to travel. In March, I took a trip with a trucker friend of mine who was taking loads all over the United States. He said he would be gone for two weeks. I decided it would be fun to go, but I never planned on more than just two weeks. We traveled to fourteen different states in four weeks. Some states, we just drove through. We stopped in Reno, Nevada, for a few nights. I was able to see a college friend, Gary Shank, who lived there. It was good to see him. I also had the opportunity to go to El Paso, Texas, to see a high school friend of mine, Jon Henry. After leaving Texas, we drove to Tucson, Arizona, for a few nights. He was not getting any loads to take back to Nebraska. By this time, I was thinking I was never going to be back in Chadron. I found out he had to take a load to Phoenix. By week three, I realized I had enough of being in a truck, and was ready to be home. After finding out I would be in Phoenix, my mom made arrangements for me to stay with my adopted grandparents, the Moons, in Mesa. I stayed with them for about four days. Besides getting to see them again, some of the highlights were going to a really neat car show. I was able to see some rare muscle cars and some real classics, like the Hudsons. My Grandpa Moon is a Hudson car collector. He has owned and sold close to a hundred Hudson cars. He knows everything about Hudsons. The other highlight was seeing an Arizona Diamondbacks baseball game. It was opening day, so Grandpa Moon took me to the game, and the Diamondbacks even won that game too. I really enjoyed the time I got to spend with them.

I later spent some time with my cousin, Rochelle, in Phoenix. I stayed with her for three days. I met her boyfriend, Brian, and he showed me around. He took me to see some sights Phoenix and I got to see the capital building and some of the sites of the big city. We cruised in his Corvette. I had a great time. The weather was awesome. I decided right then and there that when I retire, I want to live in Arizona in the winter months and be a snow bird—but only in the winter months, because my heart will always belong to Nebraska! I was very thankful to find a way back home and not be in the truck any longer. It was nice to get to visit with family. Rochelle and Brian got me a flight to Rapid City on April 11. My parents came and picked me up from the airport. Looking back on that trip now, I figured I was gone over a month and had only brought enough money for about two weeks.

When I got back from the truck trip, I was told I missed one the biggest snow storms there was. I guess Arizona was a nice place to be during that time!

I was glad to be back because I had a few wedding dances booked. That summer, I kept busy doing that. My DJ business was really starting to take off. I even went and bought an enclosed trailer to keep my equipment in. I also bought some lights to make my equipment complete.

On July 21, I had an appointment in Scottsbluff to see Dr. Packard. This time, it was a good report and he told Mom and me that I was cancer free! After all that I went through for about nine years before, my mom said that it was music to her ears to hear the words "cancer free." I was so excited to be cancer free and that my hips were no longer hurting me, I really felt like a new person with a lot to live for!

On August 3, I started my on-line classes with American Broadcasting School. To help pay for the classes, my sister, Kristin, who was one of the kindergarten teachers for Kenwood Elementary, heard about a part-time job as a paraprofessional at the school where she works. This position was working with an autistic student. I wanted something where I could work in the mornings and have my afternoon and evenings free so I could get my assignments done. I worked through the school year, and after it was over, I decided to let my sister be the teacher. I found out how hard being a teacher really was, even a teacher's aide.

On September 26, my family went to Lincoln for another Husker game. It was the three hundredth consecutive home sellout game. To honor the consecutive sellout, the Husker football team wore the uniforms from the 1962 season, when the sellout started. Nebraska won big, 55-0.

In October, I was the DJ for a wedding dance in Hot Springs, South Dakota. The next day, Josh and I left for Minnesota for another Vikings football game. We met up with his family there. We even went canoeing near his uncle's house.

Just before Christmas, Mom and I went to Scottsbluff for another checkup. This time it would be my last appointment with Dr. Packard, as he was retiring. He congratulated me for being a survivor and keeping a good attitude in spite of what I had been through. He said he felt I was truly a miracle. My checkup was the best ever and I was very thankful, but it was so hard to say good-bye to such a great doctor. It was especially hard for Mom too. She trusted him so much with my care. He truly is the best doctor ever. I hope to see him again someday, just for a visit!

Chapter 12

Now . . . There Is Even Moore to My Story

In May 2010, I graduated from American Broadcasting School. My parents hosted a cookout at my apartment and had several of my closest friends over. We had a good time celebrating! In July, it was time for my yearly PET scan, but Dr. Packard had retired. It was sad to think that he was not going to be my doctor anymore. I was happy for him to be able to enjoy some free time, but I missed him taking care of me. So I began to see Dr. Packard's nurse, Becky. After, I got a good report from her; she recommended I get a colonoscopy. She said of all the tests and surgeries that I had in the past, there was just one test I had never had done to check for any other possible cancer. In August, I had my first colonoscopy done in Scottsbluff; the scan showed two polyps, which I had removed, but lucky for me, they were benign.

When school started in the fall, I was asked to be a color commentator for the Double Q country radio station. I worked side by side with Mike Fell from Alliance, and we hosted the Friday Night Game of the Week. I really enjoyed this experience! It is exactly what I want to do. Football is my favorite sport, and radio broadcasting is my passion. For a few of the games, I was given the opportunity to do the play-by-play announcing. It was a great time for me!

Looking back on everything I have been through in the last ten years, there are many memories about my cancer experience that were no fun at all. For instance, missing out on a lot of my high school classes and activities for all of the chemotherapy treatments and the hip problems caused by the steroids. One of the worst memories I have from my doctor's visits was having spinal taps done. During the time I was taking chemotherapy to fight my cancer, I always had to have a spinal tap. I must have had close to a hundred of them. During my chemotherapy treatments in Denver, Dr. Cullen's wife, Patsy, gave me all my spinal taps. She never messed up, not even once. She told me that there was a little mole on my back that she always used as a target. She had me lie on the table and curl up in a ball. First, she would give me some sleepy medicine through my port in my chest to ease the pain, and then she would stick me with a big, long needle. Most of the time, it did not even hurt.

During my cancer treatments, I stayed really positive and kept a good attitude. I have been pretty lucky these past few years, because all my tests have come back with good reports, and no sign of *cancer*.

Cancer is still a really bad disease that kills a lot of people every day, but if you get help right away and take your treatments seriously, you have a better chance of surviving it. It is a dreaded disease that I would not wish anyone to have. It was very hard to even believe it had happened to me. As of this writing, I have had good reports with no signs of cancer for six years now!

Most recently, I have been working on promoting my DJ business, but I am currently pursuing a career in radio broadcasting. I would prefer to do sports announcing, especially football.

The radio station field may take me to a different place for a job. I might be living somewhere else for the first time in my life. My target is to still live in Nebraska, but time will tell what happens from here. I really have never wanted to live anywhere else. There's no place like Nebraska.

It has been ten years now since my first diagnosis with cancer. Through a lot of that time, things were pretty rough for me to deal with, but I also have had good things happen too. I am and always will be thankful for what I have today. I am also thankful I am able to be writing my story.

When I first learned I had cancer, I have to admit, it scared me. During that time, God provided many people in my life who were there to encourage me and pray for me. Even during some of my toughest times, I had comfort in knowing that people were praying and trusting that God would help me get through it all. The prayers are what held me up when I could not stand alone. The support I had was amazing to me. I went to all my treatments and surgeries fully supported by knowing I was in God's hands. My thanks goes out to all who cared about me. I will be forever grateful for the faith and concern of all who cared enough to pray for me. I believe in the power of prayer!

Another thing that is important is to let people know that cancer is not always bad. It is your attitude and how you deal with it that really matters and makes you stronger. You have to stay positive in order to fight it. One thing that helped me was the doctors giving me an encouraging outlook. But the most important thing for me was my faith in God and the love and support of family and friends. Cancer does not have to mean you are not going to make it. I have learned to appreciate life more and be thankful that I am healthy. I just take one day at a time and make every day count!

It is my hope that the experiences I had with my cancer, and the problems I faced, may somehow be an inspiration to others who are dealing with cancer. My best advice I could give anyone would be ***stay positive and never give up!***

Family picture taken in 2008

As of this writing, my mom was recently diagnosed with breast cancer, after a routine mammogram. It came as a shock to all of us. I made a promise to her that I would pay her back, since she was by my side through all of my cancer treatments. She never missed an appointment and always stayed with me in the hospital room throughout all my surgeries and the long rehabilitation process. With my faith in God and the love and support of family and friends, I know that I can help her to also stay positive and never give up! She is, and always will be, my hero.

Mom and I taken on her birthday in 2008

As I look back on my experience I remember how my parents tried to keep things at home as normal as possible. (We really did not know what normal was) My mom was with me on the road and to all of my doctor's appointments. My dad stayed with Kristin and worked when he was able to.

Kristin was a freshman in high school when this happened to me. She got involved in speech and even wrote a speech about my cancer. She did very well in competition and even made some of the judges cry. She gave the speech from her heart. Cancer does not just affect one person it affects a whole family. Here is a short clip from her speech.

"On a pleasant day in January, I went home after school, dreading all the home work I had. When I walked through the front door, my mom, dad, even my grandparents and some friends, just looked at me. From that moment, I knew something was terribly wrong! That's when I was told my brother had cancer, and that we had to go to Scottsbluff. I went up to my room and started to pack, and then I cried.

When I learned what cancer was, I knew that it was a very serious obstacle. Cancer is an obstacle that can be dealt with.

First of all, you have to ask yourself what is Cancer?

Cancer is one of man's most dreaded diseases, and it can attack people of all ages. Cancer is uncontrolled growth of body cells, and can have many forms.

All cancers originate in living cells, cancer cells seem to grow anywhere in the body. Cancer is not contagious; it cannot be spread from one person to another.

Cancer has often been called the "silent killer", because it gives very little or no warning of its presence in early stages.

Doctors can treat cancer by means of surgery, radiation, or chemotherapy. The choice of treatment depends on the type of cancer involved and the location of the growth in the body.

It is believed that the average person gets cancer six times a year. Their immune system destroys the cancer cells and they know nothing about it.

One million cancer cells are smaller than the head of a pin. One billion cancer cells are the size of a pea, and weigh about the same as a paper clip. This means they have the ability to float freely through the blood stream or lymph system.

On January 1, 2000, my seventeen year old brother Brad went to the hospital with a sore neck and six days later, found out it was cancer. From Gordon, he was sent to Scottsbluff to Denver and he started getting chemo in Denver. He had a real good attitude about all of this, and has taken it the best out of our whole family. I am glad that he has been positive, because with all that he has been through, I don't know if I could stay as positive as he has. Brad has gone through a lot this past year, with chemo and surgeries. He has had a rough year and I feel sorry for him, but he has taken it pretty well. The reasons he is doing so well is because of good doctors, good care, and the way he has learned to handle it.

Faith is a source of strength for many people. Some people feel that their faith has given them the strength to fight their illness, and I think that this is very true for my brother, Brad.

The family is also very important in the fight against cancer. Cancer in the family can also be confusing, scary, and lonely. Believe me; I have felt all of these feelings. Cancer is an obstacle that can be dealt with. After all, cancer is limited.

We must remember that cancer cannot: cripple LOVE, shatter HOPE, corrode FATIH, destroy PEACE, kill a FRIENDSHIP, suppress MEMORIES, silence COURAGE, invade the SOUL, steal ETERNAL LIFE, or conquer the SPIRIT."